YOUNG RIDER'S HANDBOOK
BETTER RIDING
JO BIRD

YOUNG RIDER'S HANDBOOK

BETTER RIDING

JO BIRD

Credits

T.F.H. Publications
President/CEO: Glen S. Axelrod
Executive Vice President: Mark E. Johnson
Publisher: Christopher T. Reggio
Production Manager: Kathy Bontz
US Editor: Mary E. Grangeia
Cover Design: Mary Ann Kahn

T.F.H. Publications, Inc.
One TFH Plaza
Third and Union Avenues
Neptune City, NJ 07753

ISBN 978-0-7938-3203-3

Printed and Bound in China
08 09 10 11 12 1 3 5 7 9 8 6 4 2

Library of Congress Cataloging-in-Publication Data
 Bird, Jo.
  Better riding / Jo Bird.
     p. cm.
  Includes index.
  ISBN 978-0-7938-3203-3 (alk. paper)
  1. Horsemanship. I. Title.
  SF309.B612 2008
  798.2--dc22
                              2007050740

This book has been published with the intent to provide accurate and authoritative information in regard to the subject matter within. While every reasonable precaution has been taken in preparation of this book, the author and publisher expressly disclaim responsibility for any errors, omissions, or adverse effects arising from the use or application of the information contained herein. The techniques and suggestions are used at the reader's discretion and are not to be considered a substitute for veterinary care. If you suspect a medical problem, consult your veterinarian.

The Leader In Responsible Animal Care For Over 50 Years!®
www.tfh.com

Jo Bird

Jo Bird has owned horses for most of her life and used to juggle working as a groom in the mornings and going to an office job in the afternoons! She now provides management and nutritional advice to people buying horses and has worked in an advisory capacity helping to develop new products for a leading equestrian product manufacturer. She has owned a variety of horses, from foals to aged veterans and from huge, heavy traditional cobs to fine, fit racehorses. She is the author of *Keeping a Horse the Natural Way* and *Breaking Bad Habits in Horses*.

Acknowledgments

Thanks to everyone at Sworders and to Lucy Back, Michelle Cogger, Ellen Cutlip, Katy Griffiths, Sarah Howe, Jo Jones, Laura Key, Gill Leage, Sarah Pamment, Adele Rawlinson and Gill Walker for allowing photoshoots. Thank you to my brilliant models: Kate and Lucy Fallen, Harriet de Freitas, Jenny Graham, Ellie Griffiths, Jeanette and Kelly Holzinger, Laura and James Howe, Abbey and Leah Jolliffe, Harriet and Hal Jones, Jeannie Mott, Joanna Moyers, Lotte Notley and Amber Tucker, and of course their photogenic mounts!

Contents

GETTING STARTED

If you dream of having your own horse one day, or at least of being able to ride competently, it is well worth taking time to consider where would be the best place for you to learn. Although you may know someone who has offered informally to teach you, bear in mind that they may not actually be very skilled themselves or have adequate insurance in the event that you should have an accident. After all, it is very likely that you will have a fall or two!

The following chart should help you to decide on the right place for you. Bear these questions in mind when doing your research and inquiring over the telephone or in person.

- How far away is the riding school – how would you get there?
- How much will a lesson cost, or could you offer to help there in exchange for riding tuition?
- Do they have horses or ponies suitable for your size and level of ability?
- Do they have adequate insurance and properly qualified instructors?
- Do they have an indoor or covered school in case of bad weather?
- Do they hold competitions, or provide training or horse management courses or exams?

WHAT ARE YOUR CURRENT GOALS?

- To learn basic riding skills, to be able to ride a friend's horse occasionally, or perhaps go for a ride when you are on vacation.
- To be disciplined to learn and progress to more advanced riding techniques as a hobby.
- To be able to compete in dressage/show jumping/cross-country, etc.
- To be able to go out on rides in beautiful scenery and simply enjoy time with your horse and your friends.

- To learn as much as possible about riding and horse care with a view to sharing/loaning or owning your own horse or pony.

If you know what is really important to YOU, it will help you find the most suitable training place.

It would certainly be worth taking a look at the facilities and asking if you can watch a lesson beforehand. This would give you an idea about the instructor's personality. Have a look at the horses in the stables – do they look happy, healthy, and bright eyed, or tired and skinny? Are the stables clean or deep in muck? Is there turnout so the horses can have some playtime?

Remember: If you start taking lessons somewhere but do not feel that you are progressing well enough or do not like the horses or the instructor, then try somewhere else. The aim is to enjoy a rewarding hobby and have fun, not to be unhappy doing something that you don't enjoy on a regular basis!

▲ **Take a look around** *various local riding stables, check the facilities, and meet the animals and instructor before deciding.*

◀ **Having an indoor school** *means your lessons can still proceed even in bad weather.*

◀◀ **A group lesson is** *great fun. You will have friendly competition and can learn from each other and laugh at mistakes!*

Styles of riding

There are two main styles of riding: English and Western.

In English riding the rider is taught to hold one rein in each hand and to use them independently, employing the right one to steer the horse to the right and the left one to steer him to the left. The hands are held low, just in front of the pommel (front) of the saddle, which is a low bulge just clearing the horse's withers. The stirrups are generally fairly short so that the rider's legs make an angle of about 120 degrees at the knee, and the rider's position is expected to create an imaginary straight line that stretches from ear to shoulder to hip to heel. The rider uses rein aids, leg aids, and weight aids in what are known as the four gaits (the way the horse moves), which are WALK, TROT (rising and sitting), CANTER, and GALLOP. The rider is trying to achieve absolute control and collection in each gait. Jumping is also a popular pastime in English equitation (equitation is another word meaning horse or pony riding).

Western riding was developed in the United States, Canada, and Australia to reflect the work done by cowhands on cattle ranches. In Western riding the rider holds both reins in one hand and uses the reins together rather than independently, which allows the rider to keep one hand free (originally this was done so that cowboys could use one hand to lasso cattle). The Western saddle holds the rider more securely in position than the English version. It uses a longer length of stirrup, and the legs are generally positioned further forward. There is no rising trot, and the paces are designed to be comfortable and functional: WALK, JOG, LOPE, and GALLOP. Horses are schooled for sharp turns and rapid acceleration/deceleration – skills needed when herding cattle were important. Jumping as a sport is rarely undertaken in Western riding due to the rider's position and the design of the saddle.

WHAT TO WEAR

Many establishments will hire out hats or helmets, but normally you are required to have suitable footwear at a minimum. If you decide that you will be riding regularly, it would be worth investing in some riding gear to suit the discipline in which you are most interested.

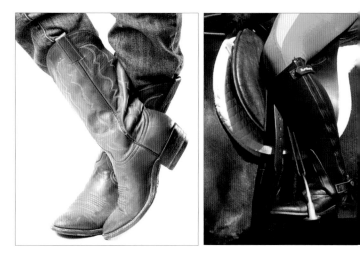

▲ **Styles of footwear** *change with the fashions, but make sure boots are sturdy and not too wide for the stirrups.*

◀▶ **A helmet or hard hat** *should be worn every time you ride. New models are lightweight.*

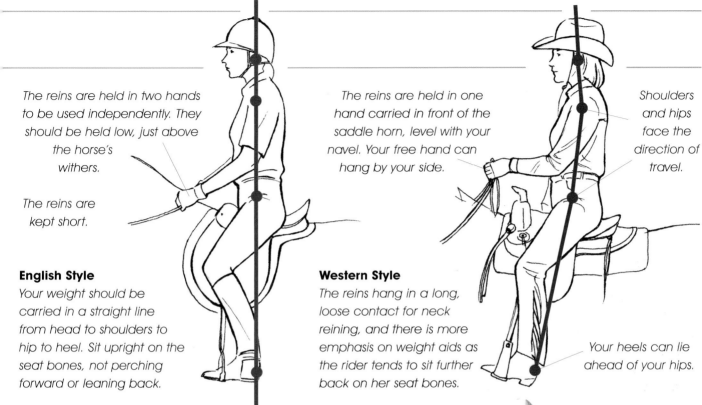

The reins are held in two hands to be used independently. They should be held low, just above the horse's withers.

The reins are kept short.

The reins are held in one hand carried in front of the saddle horn, level with your navel. Your free hand can hang by your side.

Shoulders and hips face the direction of travel.

Your heels can lie ahead of your hips.

English Style
Your weight should be carried in a straight line from head to shoulders to hip to heel. Sit upright on the seat bones, not perching forward or leaning back.

Western Style
The reins hang in a long, loose contact for neck reining, and there is more emphasis on weight aids as the rider tends to sit further back on her seat bones.

▲ **Stetsons can look very stylish.** *This young rider looks surprisingly confident in the saddle on such a large horse.*

◄ **Even casual wear should be safe.** *This rider's shoulders may get sunburned!*

SADDLERY AND TACK

Saddlery is a word used to describe the items of tack, like the saddle, bridle, reins, and stirrups, which are used to make it easier for a rider to communicate with and control a horse. They provide more comfort and stability than riding bareback.

Let's look at some common tack items you will come across and their uses. We shall begin with bridles and bits. The English bridle is shown on these pages and the Western bridle is described on pages 14 to 15.

BRIDLES

Bridles are usually made of leather, but in recent years webbing bridles have become popular for some disciplines, such as endurance, amateur racing, and also carriage driving. They come in various sizes including pony, cob, and full and are designed to fit around the contours of different sizes and builds of ponies and horses, being secure but also comfortable. The headpiece runs behind the ears and then splits to attach to the cheekpieces, which support the bit while a part known as the throatlash passes under the horse's throat. Some bridles have nosebands that may be used simply to enhance the appearance of the horse's head or as a way of altering the effect of the bit used—for example, by keeping the horse's mouth shut.

BITS

A bit is a mouthpiece to which the reins are attached. It aids the rider in controlling the horse. Most bits are made of metal (steel, nickel, brass, or copper), but some are made of rubber. There are literally hundreds of different types of bits available; they may be jointed in one or more places in the mouthpiece, or simply have a straight bar. The external sides of the bit to which the reins attach may have one or more rings or tall or short bars or shanks. Some bits have a chain that passes under the horse's jaw. Every bit purports to have a slightly different action that aims to encourage the horse to be light in the rider's hands, to raise or lower his head, or to give the rider more control – for example, if the horse tends to pull. For the sake of the horse, it is kinder to begin with a simple form of bit teamed with only a cavesson noseband, and then concentrate on improving your riding skills and communication rather than resorting to severe or restrictive gadgets to get the horse to yield. You will see riders using two reins in each hand, and these may have different effects on the action of the bit; (e.g., pelham or a gag) or the horse may be in a double bridle, which uses two bits in the horse's mouth.

GOAL: Ask an experienced person to explain the action of the bits being used on their horses or ponies.

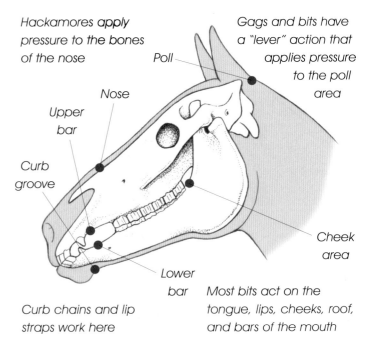

Hackamores apply pressure to the bones of the nose

Gags and bits have a "lever" action that applies pressure to the poll area

Poll

Nose

Upper bar

Curb groove

Lower bar

Cheek area

Most bits act on the tongue, lips, cheeks, roof, and bars of the mouth

Curb chains and lip straps work here

TIP Less is more. Less severe tack and more accurate riding skills will achieve far better results in the long term.

Headpiece

Browband

Cheekpiece
(top)

Noseband

Cheekpiece
(bottom)

Bit

Throatlash
(top)

Throatlash
(bottom)

Rein

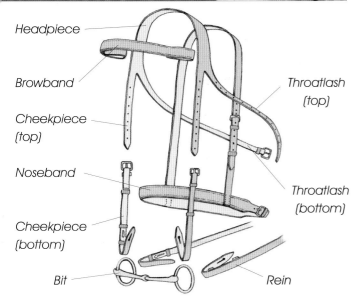

▶ **Tie-downs, martingales,** and gadgets should only be used when needed. Extra leatherwork hinders rather than helps a horse.

▲ **A bridle should be** a guiding tool not a restrictive head harness! This simple Western bridle is both kind and effective.

Putting on a bridle

Bridles generally come in three sizes: PONY, COB, and FULL. Each bridle has lots of holes punched in the leather to allow for a lot of adjustment of tightness so they are easier to fit than saddles.

   Remember to be **very** gentle when putting the bridle on. A horse has very tender skin on his face, and you need to be careful not to accidentally scratch his eyes with a buckle or a strap.

1. Stand on the left side of the horse facing forward. Undo the halter or headcollar so that it is only attached around his neck but making sure that he is still tied up.
2. Pass the reins over his head so they are in position on his neck.
3. Hold the bit flat in your left hand, and pass your right arm under his jaw to take hold of the rest of the bridle.
4. Press the bit against his lips. If he won't open his mouth, press your left thumb into the back corner of his lips and he should open his mouth. Don't worry—he has no teeth there so you won't get bitten!
5. Lift the bit high in his mouth, and pass the headpiece gently over first one ear, and then the other.
6. Make sure his mane is not caught up in the headpiece, and pull out the forelock so it lies on top of the browband.
7. The noseband should pass INSIDE the cheekpieces. Fasten it so you can slide two fingers between it and his jaw. Tuck the strap inside its keepers.
8. The throatlash is the thin long strap that passes under the jaw. You should be able to fit four fingers between the strap and the horse's cheek. Finally, check that the buckles are secured on the same holes on the left and the right sides to prevent the

bit from being lopsided. If all the straps are tucked inside their keepers, the bridle will look much tidier.

Note: Most nosebands fasten behind the bit; however, a flash, drop, or grackle may have a strap that fastens in front of the bit to prevent the horse from opening his mouth.

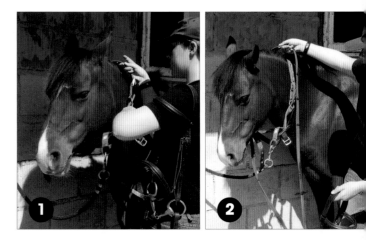

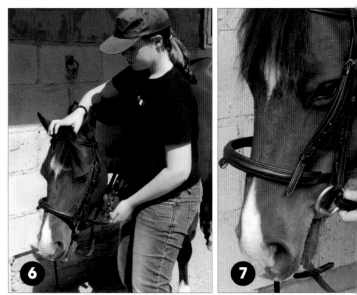

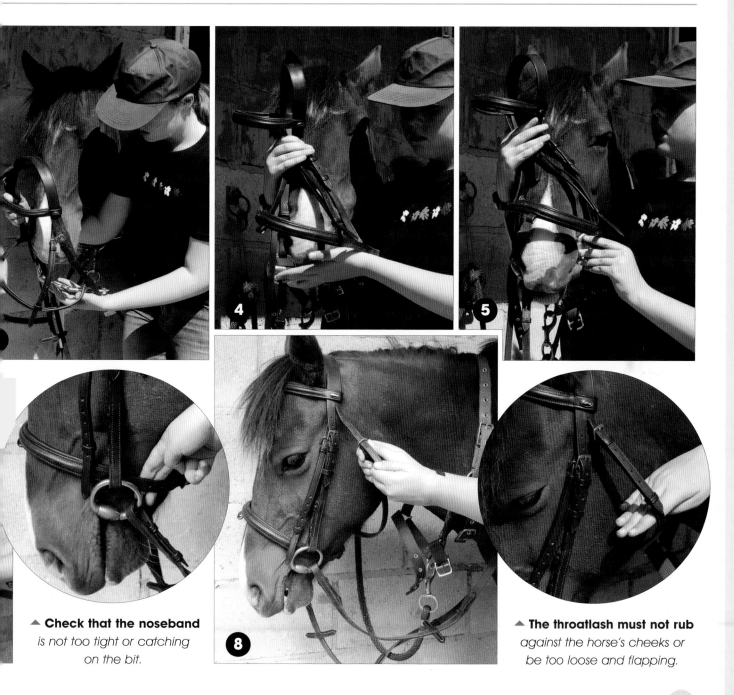

▲ **Check that the noseband** *is not too tight or catching on the bit.*

▲ **The throatlash must not rub** *against the horse's cheeks or be too loose and flapping.*

Western bridle

Western bridles come in many styles and can be very simple or very ornate. When compared to an English bridle, there are far fewer components – simply a headstall with either a full browband or commonly just a loop that fits over one of the horse's ears. Attached to this are cheekpieces that hold the bit in place. Western riders use a curb bit, which has long shanks that hang down below the jaw and to which the reins are attached. The reins are not connected into one loop but simply draped over opposite sides of the horse's neck to prevent them trailing on the ground.

HOW TO PUT ON A WESTERN BRIDLE

1. Hold the bridle in one hand, and pass your other arm under the horse's jaw.
2. Offer the bit up to the horse's mouth and put it in.
3. Reach up and gently guide one or both ears into the headstall loops, depending on the bridle.
4. Pull the forelock through the browband. If you have a throatlash, adjust it so you can fit your palm in vertically under his jaw.

A Western hackamore is a type of bitless bridle in which a rope is attached to a heavy noseband known as a bosal in order to guide the horse. Some riders prefer to use a hackamore bit because it uses pressure on the nose or the jaw created by the bosal rather than having to insert a bit into the horse's mouth.

TIP If you are using split reins, hang them over your right shoulder as you bridle up so that neither you nor the horse will step on them.

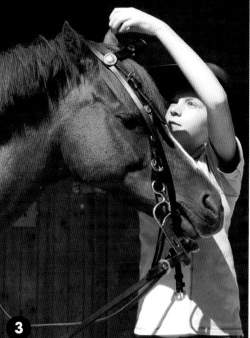

▶ **Cheekpieces** *should lie clear of the eyes, and any curb chain or strap should lie flat and loose.*

◀ **Western tack** *is designed for comfort—and carrying your ropes and bedroll too!*

Saddles

Saddles come in different styles and sizes to fit different horses and to suit different riding styles, such as for general purpose riding, dressage, or jumping.

The length of the saddle is usually measured in inches from the side of the pommel (near the brass stud) to the top center of the cantle. Pony saddles tend to be 15 to 16 in (38 to 41 cm) long and horse saddles 17 to 18 in (43 to 46 cm) long.

The width refers to the point where the pommel of the saddle sits just behind the horse's withers, so a fine-built horse with high withers is likely to need a narrow saddle and a rounder cob type may need a medium or medium-wide saddle to prevent his withers from being pinched. The panels are stuffed (known as "flocking"), but some modern saddles have air inside instead to act as cushioning.

Numnahs and saddlecloths are pads, typically made of sheepskin or fabric, that are normally used underneath a saddle for added cushioning and to soak up sweat and keep the saddle clean.

▼ **English saddles come** in different widths to fit over different withers. The length is measured diagonally from pommel to cantle (below).

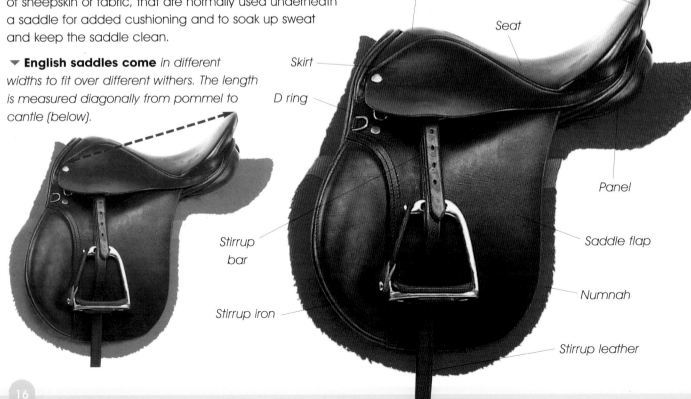

Pommel

Cantle

Seat

Skirt

D ring

Panel

Stirrup bar

Saddle flap

Numnah

Stirrup iron

Stirrup leather

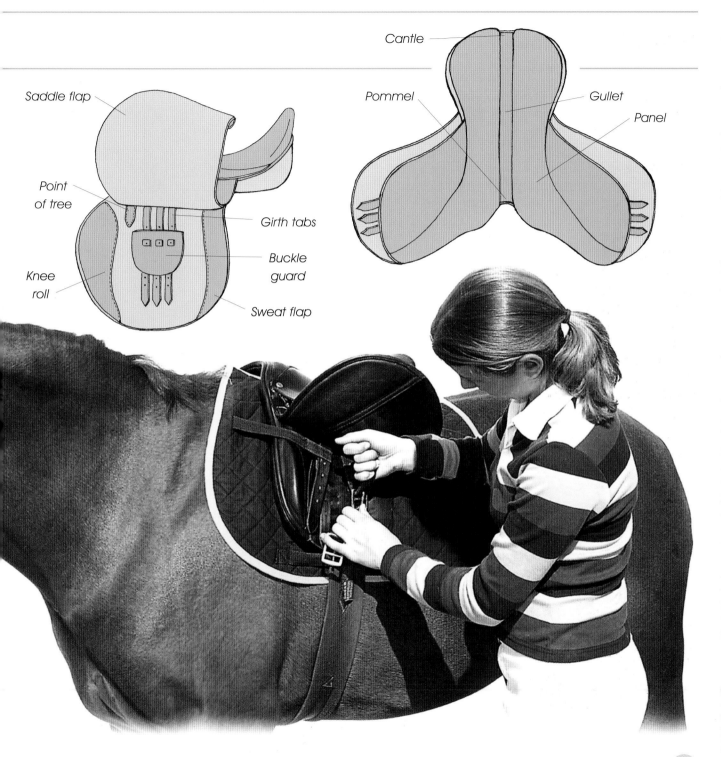

Cantle

Pommel

Gullet

Panel

Saddle flap

Point of tree

Girth tabs

Buckle guard

Knee roll

Sweat flap

Putting on a saddle

When you first start riding it is likely your horse will already be tacked up for you. But as you progress, it is useful to know how to saddle up safely.

Some saddles are heavy, so it's best to carry the saddle over one arm, with the pommel tucked into your elbow, and to support the weight with your other arm. Have the strap of the girth wrapped over the top of the saddle, not trailing along on the ground getting dirty!

1. Make sure your horse is tied up, and show him the saddle. Stand on his left side.
2. Lay the numnah or saddlecloth on his back first, high on the withers.
3. Lift the saddle high and lower it gently on top of the numnah. Slide it back to just behind the withers.
4. Pull the front of the numnah up to the highest point of the pommel or it may press down uncomfortably on the withers. The numnah may have loops that go through the girth straps, or one big loop for the girth to pass through to stop the numnah slipping back.
5. Pass the girth under the horse's belly. The girth should always be attached to the right side of the saddle (when viewed from the saddle) and be fastened and unfastened from the left side.
6. Gently tighten the girth. It is kinder to the horse if you fix it fairly loosely then tighten it in stages until it is secure enough, rather than hauling it right up all in one move.
7. Pull down the buckle guard to protect the saddle and your legs from the buckles rubbing against them.
8. Finally, run your hand just under the girth behind your horse's elbow to smooth out any creases of skin that may have developed.

▶ **It is easier to do up** *a girth with elastic end straps; this type of girth is more comfortable for the horse because it has some give in it.*

▼ **Support the saddle** *with both arms or you risk damaging it and yourself!*

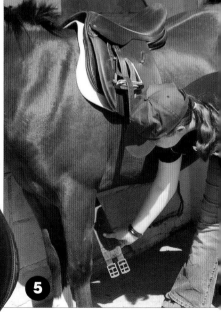

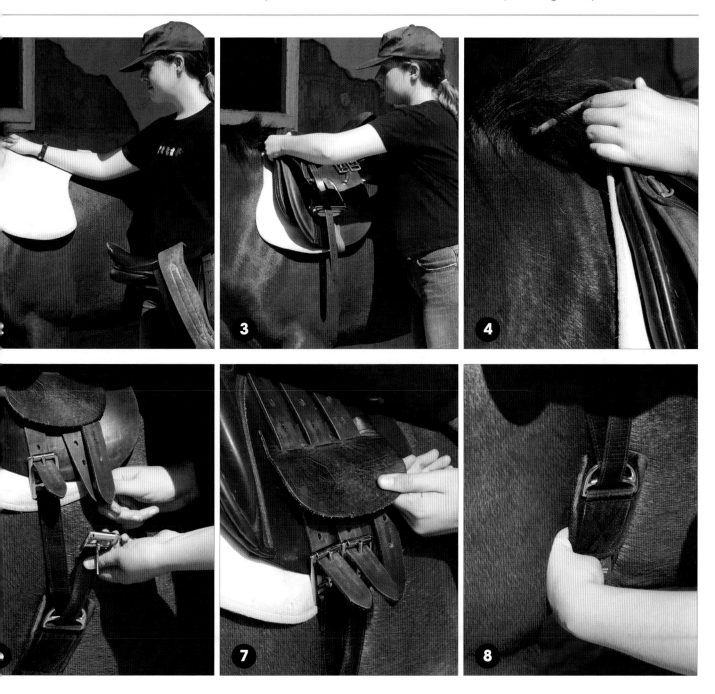

Western tack

WESTERN SADDLE

A Western saddle is wide and designed so that it can be used on a variety of horses rather than always needing expert fitting to each horse, as an English saddle does. The underside is usually covered in sheepskin, and it is used with a thick saddle blanket to help keep the horse comfortable. It has a high horn at the front, which was designed for helping the rider to hold on to roped cattle or as a tie point when using a horse to carry dead stock or supplies on his back. The presence of this horn and also a high cantle at the back certainly makes the rider feel secure because there is plenty to hold onto!

The stirrup leathers have "fenders" that provide a flat surface against which your legs lie and that help prevent pinching from the leathers. The stirrups themselves are a much wider style than European irons and are usually made of wood covered in leather. A western girth is called a cinch, and it is often made of string, woven hair, cord, or leather.

TACKING UP WESTERN-STYLE

1. Place your pad or blanket forward, and slide it back into position.
2. Gently lower the saddle down onto the pad and drop the cinch down.
3. Pass the strap (latigo) on the left side of the saddle through the metal loop of the cinch.

Horn

Fork (swell)

Front jockey and seat jockey

Cantle

Back housing (back jockey)

Skirt

Latigo carrier

Leather or webbing strap (latigo)

Fender

String cinch

Buckle

Stirrup keeper

Stirrup

Blanket or pad

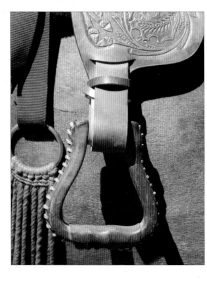

▲ **Many types of saddle** exist. Equitation saddles have deeper seats, roping saddles have stirrups hung further forward, and barrel racing saddles are short with a rounded skirt.

TIP If you find it difficult to tie your cinch tight enough using a latigo knot, use a cinch with a buckle at both ends, which can be tightened while on horseback.

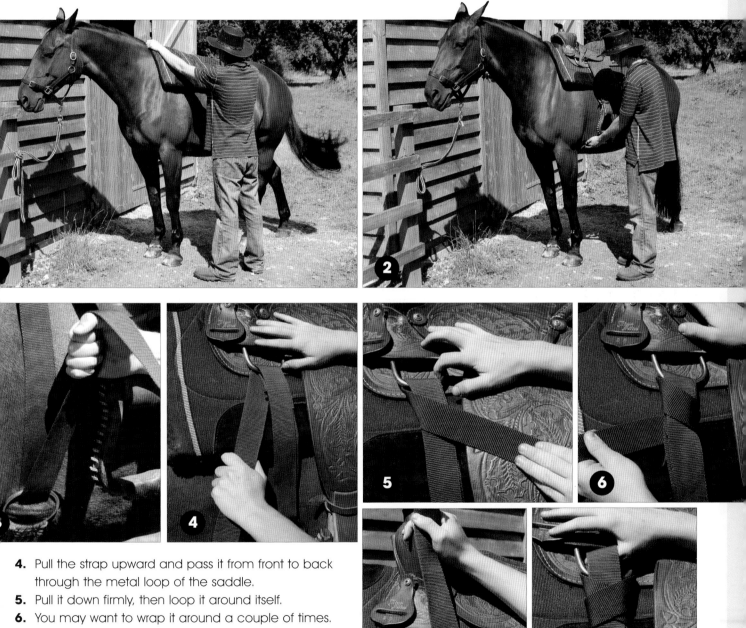

4. Pull the strap upward and pass it from front to back through the metal loop of the saddle.
5. Pull it down firmly, then loop it around itself.
6. You may want to wrap it around a couple of times.
7. Pass it up through the saddle ring from below.
8. Poke the strap through the loop to secure the knot.

Stirrups

Stirrups are very important because they help you to feel secure in the saddle. If your stirrups are too long, you will be constantly reaching for them and find it hard to keep your feet securely in them. If they are too short, they will make you sit too heavily in the saddle and you will find it hard to adjust your weight or to do a rising trot comfortably.

From the ground, you can make a good guess at the length of stirrup that will suit you by aligning the stirrup leather with your arm, with your fingers placed by the top stirrup bar. The base of your stirrup should reach just to your armpit (*pictured below*).

▲ **Compare these stirrup lengths:** *too long and you risk losing them, too short and your legs will ache. At the correct length you will feel safe and balanced.*

ADJUSTING YOUR STIRRUPS IN THE SADDLE

For a normal length of stirrup as used in English riding, the bottom of the stirrup iron should be in line with your ankle bone. Don't panic if your stirrups are wrong or not level and there is no one to help you adjust them. You can learn how to do this on your own.

1. Tie your reins in a loop or hold them in one hand. Keep both feet in your stirrups but put your weight into the one that you are not planning to adjust. Reach down and pull upward on the strap that needs adjusting to release the pin from the buckle.

2. Slide the leather to the correct length by either pulling up to shorten it or pushing down with your foot in the stirrup to lengthen it.

3. Press the buckle pin into the correct hole (you will be able to do this by feel alone after some practice), then slide the underneath of the stirrup leather so that the buckle is lying back up by the stirrup bar.

ADJUSTING THE GIRTH FROM THE SADDLE

Quite often the saddle needs retightening once you have been riding for a few minutes. Your weight may have pushed the saddle down or your horse has relaxed, which has made the girth loose. Make sure your horse is standing calmly, and hold the reins in one hand.

1. Reach down and lift up the saddle flap. Keep your leg forward and use it to keep the saddle flap out of the way.

2. Pull up one girth strap at a time to tighten them, checking that the buckles are safely secured in the new holes.

3. Feel how tight the girth is by sliding your fingers under it, and retighten if necessary.

TIP Stirrup leathers often have numbers stamped next to the holes. If you often ride the same horse, learn which number hole offers the right length for you.

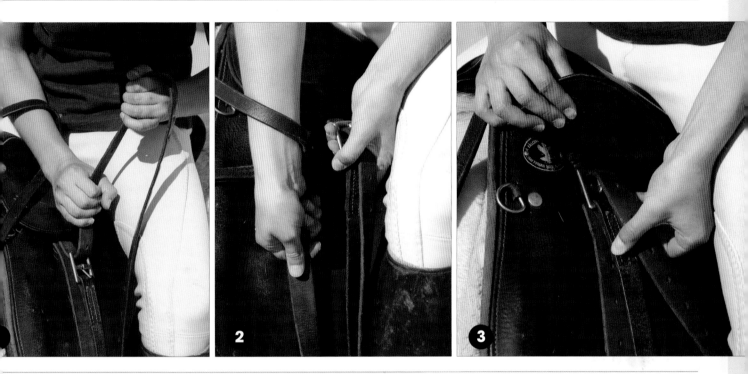

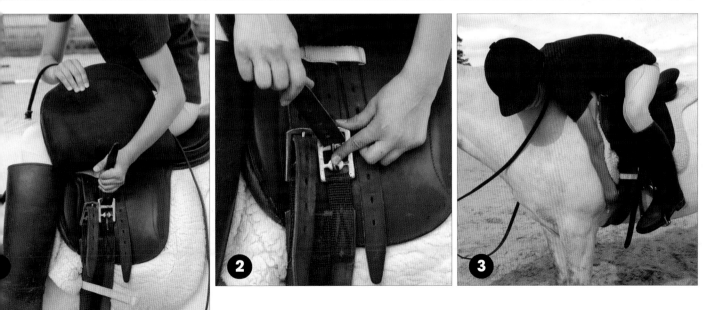

MOUNTING AND DISMOUNTING

Mounting is the term used for getting on a horse. It is useful to learn to mount from the ground (which can be tricky if you have a tall horse), but you can also mount using a mounting block or with the aid of someone else giving you a "leg up." **Before mounting, always check that your girth is tight!** If your saddle slips as you are trying to get on your horse's back, you could have a nasty accident.

MOUNTING FROM THE GROUND

1. Stand by your horse's left (near side) shoulder facing toward his rear. Hold both reins in your left hand to stop him from walking off, and hold the stirrup in your right hand with the back edge of it turned forward.
2. Place your left foot in the stirrup (you need to be supple!), and hop around so you are facing his side. Make sure you do not poke the horse with your toe or he may see this touch as a cue to move off.
3. With your left hand, hold the reins and a chunk of mane or the pommel of the saddle. Hold the far side of the saddle with your right hand.
4. Do a final hop and spring up, pushing your weight up into your left foot, which is in the stirrup iron.
5. Straighten your left leg and swing your right leg over the horse's back, being careful not to kick him.
6. Sit down **gently** in the saddle and put your right foot in the stirrup. You may need to look down and guide it in with your hand to check that the leather is not twisted.

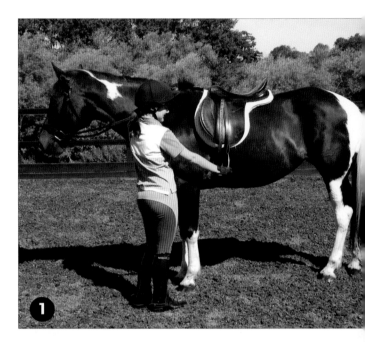

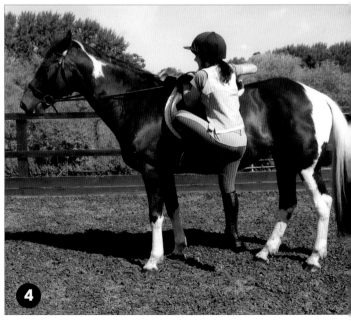

TIP Ask someone to pull down on the stirrup on the opposite side as you mount – it will stop the saddle from slipping as you put your weight on the left stirrup.

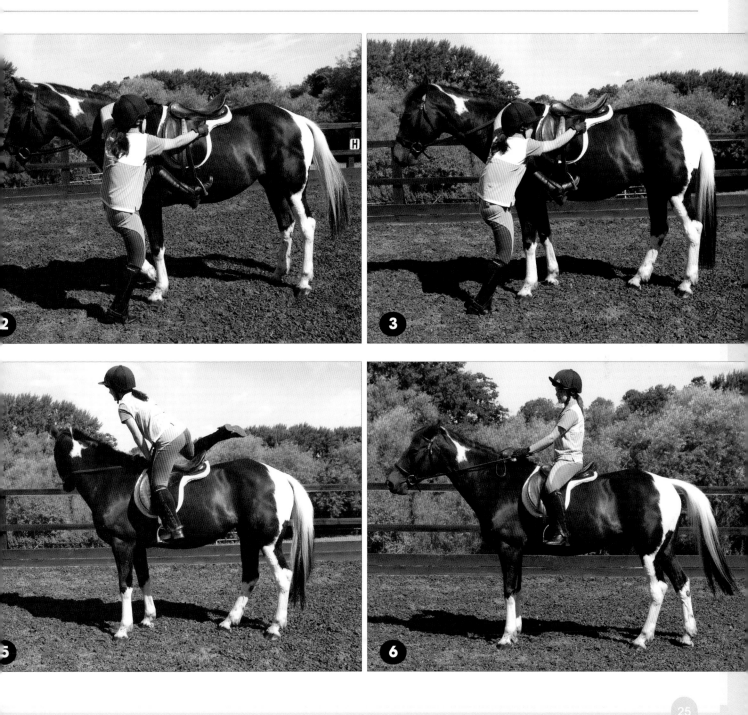

Using a mounting block

Mounting blocks are useful if you have a tall horse or if your saddle is liable to slip. It gives you added height so you do not need to haul yourself up by hanging on to the saddle. The hardest part is often trying to get your horse to stand close enough to it!

GETTING A LEG UP

This is useful when you cannot reach your stirrup from the ground or you are riding bareback. There is a knack to getting the timing right, so it may take a little practice.

1. Face the side of the horse, and hold your reins in your left hand with your right hand on the saddle.
2. Bend your left leg out behind you. Your helper should hold your knee and leg with both hands.
3. Decide between you on the moment when you should spring up (such as on the count of "One, Two, Three"). Then you should leap as your helper lifts you up and swing your leg over the horse's back.
4. Lower yourself into position in the saddle.

Caution Some people are stronger than you think – I have known people propelled into the air so hard that they fly over the horse completely!

GOAL: Learn how to give a friend a leg up.

▲ **Using a mounting block** *helps to stop the saddle from slippir*

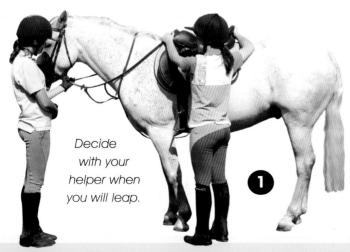

Decide with your helper when you will leap.

1

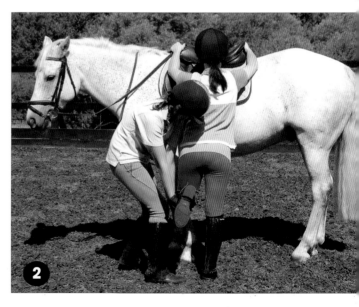

2

TIP If your horse has a tendency to nip you as you mount, keep the outside rein a little shorter so his head is turned slightly away from you.

▲ **Left toe** *in the stirrup.* ▲ **Hop up** *and swing your leg over.* ▲ **Gently lower** *yourself into position.*

Dismounting

Dismounting means getting down off your horse. Before you dismount, make sure that your horse is standing still, and look down to see where your feet will land – you don't want to drop into a puddle or a pile of droppings!

1. Take **both** feet out of the stirrups. Do not be tempted to leave your left foot in the stirrup because you risk being dragged behind should your horse move off unexpectedly.
2. Hold the reins in your left hand and the pommel of the saddle with your right hand.
3. Lean forward and swing your right leg over the horse's back (taking care not to knock him).
4. Slide down and land on both feet, bending your knees slightly to cushion the impact.

Once dismounted, you should **run up your stirrups** before leading the horse or taking off the tack. This prevents the stirrups from banging loose on the horse's sides, which could upset him. Also, if you try to carry a saddle with the stirrups down they can easily get caught up or the irons can knock against you.

1. Hold the stirrup leather with one hand. Slide the iron up the back of the leather as high as you can.
2. Take hold of the leather and thread it through the iron.
3. The horse is ready to be led safely or untacked now.
4. You should also **take the reins over the horse's head** if you are leading him from the ground.

TIP Do **not** be tempted to keep one foot in the stirrup and climb down. If your horse moves off, you could easily be dragged.

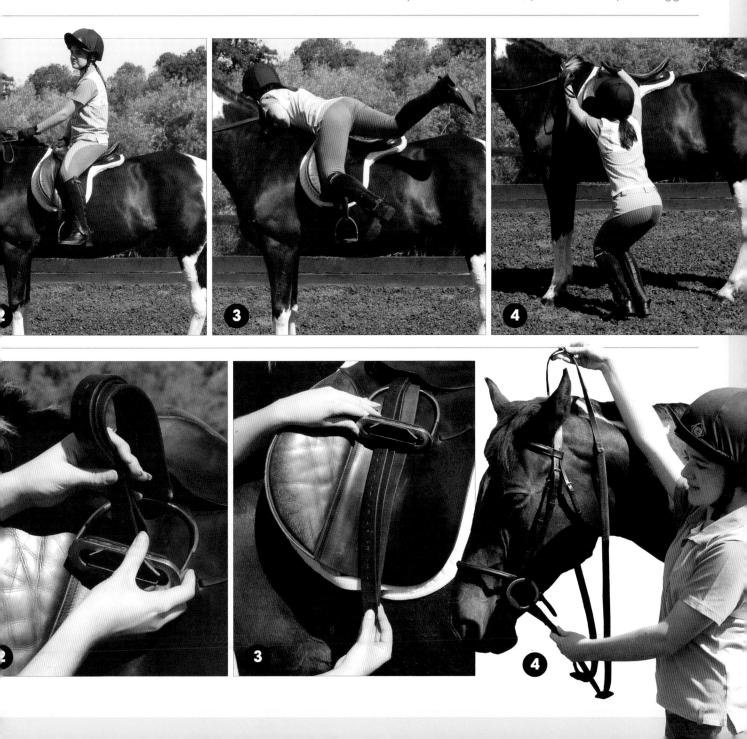

Holding the reins correctly

The reins are a direct link of communication from the horse's head to your hands. It is for this reason that you should try to imagine a line from the horse's mouth, along each rein, through your hand and wrist, and ending at each of your elbows. As the horse moves, try to maintain this light but direct contact because any interruption in this line – for example, if you have loose flapping reins or deliver a sudden jerk to the horse's mouth – will upset his rhythm and balance.

In the English style of equitation, each rein should pass from the bit between the rider's little finger and ring finger, through the hand, and out over the first finger with the thumbs on top.

▲ A good hand position *and a sensitive contact on the bit will help you communicate with your horse and achieve balanced paces.*

◀ The rein enters *between the third and little fingers, passes up through the palm of the hand, and is held in place by the thumb.*

▲ Western riders *generally hold both reins in one hand, keeping the thumb uppermost. Bend your arms at the elbow, and carry your rein hand just in front of the horn.*

◀ Keep your reins *the same length and your hands parallel to each other. This rider has no "feel," and the horse will not understand what is expected of him.*

TIP To shorten your reins, take them both in one hand and then slide the free hand forward. Hook the thumb of this hand over the second rein and move your second hand up too.

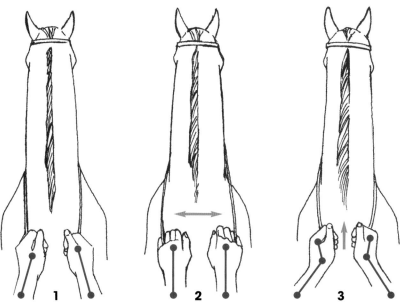

1. The correct position is with the thumbs on top and a straight line from bit to fingertips to wrist to elbow. The elbow acts as a shock absorber, so there is no unintentional rein resistance.

2. This is wrong. To be correct, a rider should imagine he is holding the reins like holding two cups of coffee. Keep the hands about 5 in (13 cm) apart (just wider than the horse's bit).

3. This is a broken axis. There is tension in the wrists, which breaks the straight line from the bit to the elbow. As a result, the sensitivity of communication with the horse is lost.

▼ **These reins are far too long!** *The rider has no powers of steering, and the horse just stops through the lack of communication despite the rider's kicks of encouragement.*

CHAPTER FOUR

UNDERSTANDING YOUR HORSE

Riding is about communication and the partnership that is formed between you and your horse. Not only do you want to be sympathetic in the signals you give to him, but it helps to be able to pick up on the signals that your horse is giving back to you.

Signs of discontentment or fear:

- Ears flat back
- Swishing tail or tail clamped down
- Whites of the eyes showing
- Tension in the back
- Stamping legs
- Kicking out
- Nipping and biting
- Pulling down on the reins
- Head shaking
- Snorting or flared nostrils
- Fidgeting or running backwards

▼ **The resistance** *in this horse is an obvious sign of displeasure.*

Signs of contentment:

- Ears forward or flicking forward and back
- Loose, swinging tail
- Friendly eyes
- Suppleness in the back
- Relaxed, swinging stride
- Soft, responsive mouth
- Calm but keen attitude
- General willingness
- Acceptance of your aids

▶ **Happy horses and riders** – *these horses walk with a swinging gait and relaxed tails, and an ear flicking now and then to monitor the world around them.*

TIP Never punish your horse because trauma in his past may be the cause of anxiety in certain situations. Horses are seldom naughty; there are reasons for their behavior.

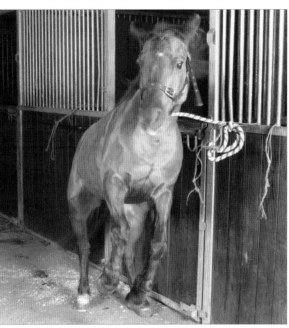

◀◀◀ **A horse that naps** is not simply naughty – he fears leaving the security of his companions.

◀◀ **Showing the whites** of the eyes is a sign of fear or discontent. Here, the buzz and vibration of electric clippers is frightening to him.

◀ **The restraint of being tied up** can cause distress. If startled, a horse's natural desire is to run away, but being tied up prevents him doing so.

◀ **Love of life** is expressed by the exuberance of this horse.

▲ **Show love and compassion** and you will be rewarded with a true friend.

Approaching a horse

When you greet any horse, talk to him and approach him slowly and walk toward his shoulder with your arm outstretched to offer him the back of your hand to sniff. Be careful not to wave your arms around because it could alarm him and he might back away from you.

Never approach a horse from behind and go near his hindquarters or pat his rump. He may not have seen you and may kick out in surprise!

MAKING FRIENDS

Horses have days when they are not feeling their best, just as we do; but if bad behavior or apparent discomfort persists, then ask for help in identifying the cause. Perhaps the bit is hanging too low in the horse's mouth or the noseband is pinching. Has the horse had his teeth checked recently? Sharp or split teeth are a common problem. Maybe there is a girth gall (a painful lump caused by sweating and rubbing around the girth area), or your aids are just confusing him and he is becoming frustrated.

If you are angry or upset yourself, it is easy to blame your horse when things don't go right and perhaps be overly brutal with your aids. Take a few deep breaths, think "calm," and stroke your horse's neck to create a better mood.

▶ **Stroking and talking** *to a horse can help to calm him. Make sure you stroke **not slap**, which is not nice!*

▶▶ **Simple checks,** *for instance for girth galls, can identify reasons why your horse might be grumpy.*

TIP By grooming and stroking, you can discover where your horse loves to be scratched. He will mouth with his lips, and by scratching these places, you can make him putty in your hands!

◀ **Tenderness goes a long way** *to making friends. Also, try blowing up their nostrils because it is a good way for them to take in your scent.*

◀◀ **Approach a horse** *from the side. Walk confidently but with arms and eyes lowered. This is horse language for "Look, I am a friend."*

▼ **Mutual grooming** *is what trusted companions do. By observing horses, you can mimic their behavior to communicate with them better.*

Swinging the lead rope will send him away!

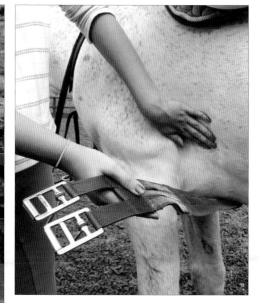

EFFECTIVE AIDS

Aids are a rider's means of communicating with the horse. You can "whisper" using a gentle squeeze on the reins or by closing the lower leg, or "shout" by kicking or pulling. A good rider learns to refine his or her aids so that the horse understands clearly without constant nagging or bullying.

NATURAL AIDS

Natural aids are things that a person is naturally equipped with: the voice, hands, weight/seat, and legs.

Voice

Using your voice can help in a variety of ways. Many horses are longed to exercise them from the ground from a long lead rope, and they learn voice commands, such as "Trot on" or "Whoa" while exercising in this way. It is useful to use the same commands with some horses so they recognize familiar instructions when being ridden, especially if your leg and rein aids are not very accurate!

If you are trying to liven up your horse and create a faster stride or more impulsion, then use an upbeat, lively tone of voice in a higher pitch, such as "T-rot on."

If you are trying to slow your horse down or help to calm a grumpy, uncooperative animal, speak slowly in an exaggerated deeper tone, such as "Woooaaah."

Hands

Humans are lucky to have the benefit of hands (rather than hooves or paws) because they are incredibly flexible and sensitive parts of our bodies. Your hands are the link between you and the mouth of the horse, another highly sensitive area, so it is important to be sympathetic with your use of the reins. Not only is it important to use each hand independently, but you should also be able to alter the tension on the reins by opening and closing individual fingers. As the horse moves, his neck stretches forward

and gets longer, lifting and falling in relation to his gait. It is important to move your hands slightly forwards and backwards in time with this movement to avoid pulling him in the mouth and causing him to tense and fix his neck in an effort to avoid any pain.

▶ **No booting!** *Start with gentle, "quiet" aids that gradually get stronger if you are ignored.*

▼ **A good rider** *has sensitive hands. At the walk, move your hands forward and back to allow the neck to stretch.*

TIP A horse knows he is doing the right thing because the rider does nothing. Do not nag with legs or hands; if the horse is correct, his reward is that you are **still**.

Voice can be used both to calm and to encourage your horse, depending on the tone you use.

Hands should be light and giving; they act to harness energy and then channel it through sensitivite direction – not by restriction.

▶ **Horse and rider harmony** is created when clear instructions invite the correct response from the horse. Horses really want to please!

Seat can be lightened or tensed to allow the horse's back to lift or to drive him forward or block energy.

Weight is the core of your balance and can be used for creating lateral as well as forward/back motion.

Legs They define instructions and should wrap around the horse, but remain still unless you are instigating a request.

▲ **Teaching voice commands** is a good communication tool, both when longeing and during ridden work.

Weight / seat

The term "seat" refers to how your weight is passed from your upper torso into the saddle. You may have a light seat with your weight predominantly passing through your spine and hips and into your legs and stirrups, or a heavy seat where your legs are light and the weight is predominantly passing from your torso into the saddle through your buttocks. Both are used to fine-tune instructions to the horse. It is very important to stay central in the saddle, unless you intend to alter your horse's balance.

Lateral (sideways) movements

Imagine that you are carrying someone on your shoulders – if they lean to the right you will become unbalanced and risk toppling over, unless you move to the right so that you are directly underneath them again. In the same way, if you put all your weight on your right seat bone, it will encourage the horse to move over to the right to be directly underneath the weight that he is feeling.

Forward movements

Leaning very slightly back, with your weight directly pushing evenly through your seat bones, often encourages a faster pace.

Backward movements

When asking for rein-back, it is important to lighten your seat to allow the horse to round his back to be able to take a step back.

Experiment: Try crawling on all fours and get someone to sit on your back. Move forward a few paces. Now ask them to sit further over to one side, and then feel the difference and note how you have to move to compensate for the uneven weight distribution.

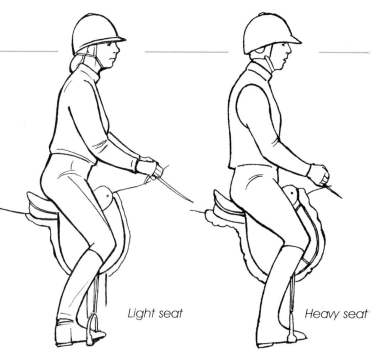

Light seat   *Heavy seat*

▲ **A light seat** *allows your horse to lift his back when going over poles or being asked to rein-back.* **A heavy or collapsed** *seat can block his freedom of movement.*

▲ **Feel what it is like** *to be a horse and how your own balance is influenced by the position of your rider!*

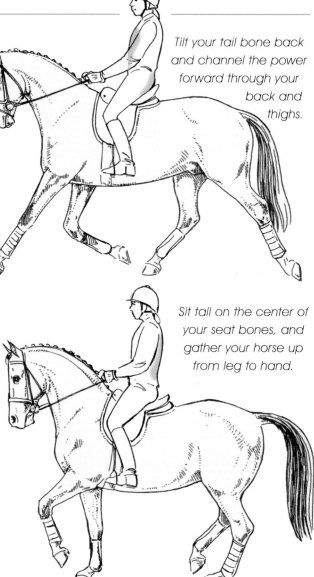

Tilt your tail bone back and channel the power forward through your back and thighs.

Sit tall on the center of your seat bones, and gather your horse up from leg to hand.

▲ **Having a balanced seat** *and flexible hips and back will enable your horse to move freely under you.*

▶ **Being even slightly lop-sided** *can create problems, like uneven muscle tone, bruising, or stiffness.*

▲ **These diagrams show** *just how much your weight can influence the direction and speed of a horse. By watching and talking to experienced dressage riders, you can learn so much about communication skills.*

Legs

Do not grip with your knees thinking it will make you more secure in the saddle because you will actually become too rigid and are likely to bounce around more. Your legs act as shock absorbers, so keeping your knees relaxed means your lower legs will be more flexible. Not only will you be more secure in the saddle, but you will be able to move them sympathetically and effectively to guide the horse. Keep your weight down into the stirrups so that, if your horse shies, you can push down on them to keep your balance rather than being tipped forward.

Your horse will feel the pressure and positioning of your legs, so it is crucial to understand what your leg aids mean. A horse that receives random kicks from the rider will get confused and become deadened to the leg because the instructions are meaningless and merely serve to irritate him.

Both legs squeezing together. This indicates to the horse that you wish him to step forward.
One leg squeezing. This indicates to the horse that you want the horse to move sideways away from your leg.

Combining the aids.
Leg aids can be further refined when used in connection with other aids, e.g., the hands and seat. For example, the aids to rein back involve asking the horse to move forward by squeezing with both legs but preventing forward movement by restricting rein contact and then channeling the energy backward by lightening your seat.

ARTIFICIAL AIDS

These are designed to be used as an extension of our own natural aids in order to amplify or make clearer our commands. Artificial aids include whips and spurs, but these should only be used by experienced riders. The whip should only be used as an extension of your own leg aid and be applied in the same position on the girth area. One tap with the whip is sometimes preferable to the horse receiving constant nagging and kicking by the rider trying to liven him up. Spurs should only be used by the most experienced adult riders, and their use should be so light as to be almost undetectable to an onlooker. In some showing classes "dummy" spurs can be used; these give the appearance of spurs but without the severity of their action.

TIP: Your aids are there to direct and alter what the horse is doing. If he is doing what you ask, then the best reward for him is for you to stay still and not fiddle with the reins or alter rein or leg pressure. Only give an aid if it is needed, and then release the pressure as soon as it is heeded and your horse has done what you asked of him. *A nagging rider produces an unresponsive horse.*

HOW TO BECOME A REALLY GOOD RIDER

Try to understand your horse, and treat every animal you ride as an

◄ **Yee ha!** *A wild use of legs and this rodeo horse is really flying!*

TIP Use the lightest possible aid to start with, only increasing it if you get no response. **Ask**, then **tell**, then **demand**!

individual. Listen carefully to your instructor, and ask him/her questions. If you understand the logic behind, for example, **why** squeezing with your legs is a better solution than hauling on the reins to bring up a horse's head, then you will become a real rider rather than just a robot.

▶ **Be accurate with your aids.** *Use your leg **on** the girth for impulsion, **behind** the girth to control the quarters for bending and lateral work, and **further back** for canter strike-offs and flying changes. Dressage riders also advance their leg to encourage extension.*

◀ **Your legs should be relaxed** *and wrap around the horse. Do not grip with your knees, but let your weight sink down into your seat and heels so that your lower legs are relaxed and loose and so able to move independently.*

▶ **A whip should not** *flap around or interfere with the rein contact. Ride with it lying across your thigh, and only use it where you would use your leg – **only** use it to reinforce a leg aid and not as a form of punishment.*

TRANSITIONS

When your instructor mentions a "transition," he or she is talking about the stage in between two different gaits. **Upward** transitions are those that take you from a slower to a faster pace, for example, from HALT to WALK, WALK to TROT, and TROT to CANTER. It is also possible to do a transition from HALT or WALK straight into CANTER. **Downward** transitions are those that diminish speed: CANTER to TROT or TROT to WALK, for example.

▲ **Even when slowing down,** *you must ride **from your leg into your hands***. *Simply hauling on the reins won't do!*

▲ **Allow your hands to go forward** *as you step up a pace and hold them static to restrain the movement for a downward transition.*

The goal of a good rider is to try to achieve smooth transitions so that one pace flows into the next, whether it be upward or downward. Slowing down requires aids that limit the forward movement, and this is done by closing your hands and therefore restricting the horse with your reins.

With all downward transitions, it is important to maintain a contact with your horse's sides and still squeeze slightly with your legs, but to restrict the forward movement with your hands. The impulsion (power) will then come from his hind legs as if to move forward, but be captured at the bit with your restricting rein contact;

he should slow down smoothly. If you only pull on the reins, the horse is likely to pull on your hands and you will start a battle!

FROM HALT TO WALK

You want your horse to stand still and calmly in halt – but not to fall asleep! Before attempting to move off, establish a contact on the reins so your horse knows you are about to ask him to do something. Squeeze with both your heels just behind the girth area. As soon as you feel your horse attempting to take a step forward, move your hands slightly forward so that he can stretch out his neck. If your aids are correct, he will move freely into walk. As he walks along, try to feel the movement underneath you and relax your seat and hands so you follow this movement.

GOAL: Try to feel how each leg moves as your horse walks around the arena.

TIP The half-halt (see page 88) is a good movement to learn—it allows your horse a stride's warning, which will result in more accurate transitions.

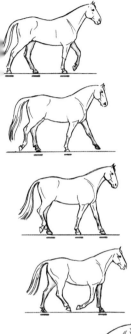

◀ **The walk is a four-beat pace** – *the hooves are planted in succession e.g., right hind, right fore, left hind, left fore as can be seen from the diagram.*

SOLVING PROBLEMS: MY HORSE WILL NOT BUDGE!

Either

Your horse is lazy or he is not sensitive to your leg aid. Use a stronger leg aid backed up by your voice aid as you command "Walk on."

Or

Your horse is confused about what you are asking him to do. Make sure your rein contact is not too short and restricting him from being able to walk forward freely.

◀ **Is your horse slow** *because he is in pain, overweight, or unfit? Consider the cause before bullying him into action with your legs. For a horse that plants his feet, try pulling on one rein and using one leg to turn him in a very tight circle. Often this is just enough to get him to rebalance and "un-set" his feet!*

▲ **Give and take** *with the reins and keep your hips fluid so they can accommodate the motion. Restricting with rein or seat will shorten the stride.*

▲ **To ask for walk** *from a halt, gather your reins, squeeze with both legs, and immediately allow for forward motion with your fingers on the reins.*

Walk to trot

Get an active walk, then sit deep in the saddle and squeeze with your legs. If there is no response, give two taps with both heels behind the girth. Keep your heels down or your weight will tip forward. As your horse goes forward in the transition, remember to allow more rein with your hands. However, once in trot, the horse's frame is more compact than in walk, so you may find you have to shorten your reins again.

Trot is probably the hardest pace to master. It is a two-beat gait and feels very different to ride when condensed into shorter strides (collected) or ridden with lengthened strides (extended). You will probably learn "working" trot, which is somewhere in between the two and is the pace that your horse will naturally take.

RISING TROT
Trotting can feel very bouncy, and you may feel unsafe in the saddle at first. Learning to rise to the rhythm of the trot will not only make you more comfortable, but your horse will be less tired from having to cope with your weight bouncing about on his back.

SITTING TROT
To be able to sit to the trot, you need to slow the trot down and sit deep in the saddle. Do not tense up or you will bounce around; instead try to loosen your stomach muscles so you can follow the movement of the horse.

THE TROT DIAGONAL
When performing rising trot, it is usual to be aware of whether you are on the right or left diagonal. You want to "sit" every time the horse's outside foreleg moves backwards.

If you are riding a change of rein or figure eight at trot, you will need to change the diagonal each time you change direction. This is usually done at the point X in the center of the arena (see page 56 for a diagram of arena markings). Simply sit for an extra beat and then carry on rising and siting. Look down to your outside to check whether you are now siting in time with your horse's outside leg coming back under you.

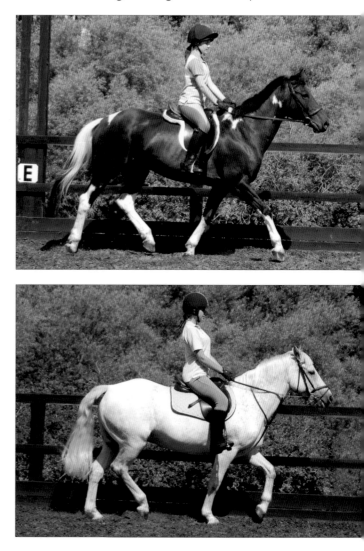

TIP Remember to change the hand your whip is in each time you change your diagonal. It should always be held in your inside hand and lie neatly across the top of your knee.

▼ **Rising trot is less tiring** *for both horse and rider. In sitting trot (bottom), the rider must relax the seat and back and allow them to undulate with the motion.*

▶ **The trot is a two-beat pace** *in which the horse's legs move in sync with one another in diagonal pairs.*

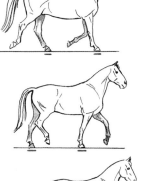

▲ **If you change the rein,** *remember to change your diagonal in rising trot at point X in the arena. You should be sitting as the new outside shoulder moves back toward you.*

Cantering

The canter is a three-beat gait with one foot coming down, then a diagonal pair, and finally the last foot. There is a moment when all four legs are off the ground before the next stride begins. If you are cantering around an arena or on a circle, the aim is to have the inside foreleg as the leading leg. This means the shoulder and leg movement on the inside will appear to stretch farther in front of the other foreleg. If you watch other people riding, you should be able to spot this. When you are on board, you can glance down to see if you have your horse on the correct leg and, in time, you will learn to recognize if you are right just by the way the horse feels under you.

THE AIDS FOR CANTER

Begin with a strong, steady, rhythmic trot. Do not let your horse rush.

To canter on the right rein

- Sit up tall and deep in the saddle (sit as if you were doing rising trot).
- Pick a corner of the arena where you are going to ask for canter and just tweak the outside rein to signify you are going to ask the horse to do something, then release.
- Put your outside (left) leg behind the girth and squeeze, then squeeze your right leg on the girth area.
- Steer your horse around the corner and keep the inside leg pressure on if you feel him falling in on the circle. Keep the pressure on the outside leg if he is tempted to slow down back into trot again.
- Once in a good rhythm, check if your horse is on the correct leading leg. If not, bring him back into trot and ask again at the next corner.

For a downward transition back into trot, increase the rein contact (especially the outside rein), tense your back, and sit deep to block the movement of the horse.

▲ **Sit up and look** in the direction of travel. An active but steady trot will enable a smooth strike-off into canter.

▼ **This diagram** shows the aids for cantering on the left rein.

▼ **Whichever rein** you are on, the inside shoulder should appear more advanced if you are on the correct leg.

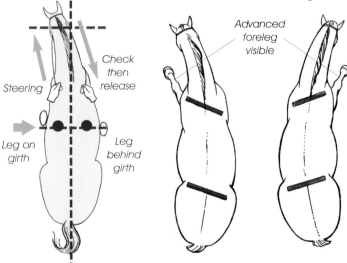

Steering

Check then release

Leg on girth

Leg behind girth

Advanced foreleg visible

TIP Keep your reins fairly short and sit upright. If you lean forward or your reins are too loose, your horse will not canter but just run and get faster and faster in trot—not very comfortable!

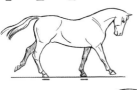

▶ **Controlling the speed** *will create a rhythmic and more comfortable canter.*

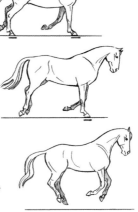

▶ **The canter** has three distinct beats beginning with one hindleg, a hind and a fore together, and finally the leading fore.

Riding Western style

The aim of a Western-trained horse is to be able to work at speed, with a swift turn of foot and the agility to enable him to turn or stop in an instant.

Whereas in English riding you hold one rein in each hand and have a fairly short contact, Western riding encourages free self-carriage of the horse in a more extended outline. The rider carries both reins in one hand. The technique – known as "neck reining" – means that in order to go left you move your hand to the left. The horse feels the right rein brush against his neck and moves away from it, thus going to the left. The reins hang down from a long rein contact so there is minimal influence from the rein, with pressure being exerted on the bit only if the movement is exaggerated. A horse trained in the English way would certainly find this confusing, and feeling pressure on the right would almost certainly make him turn right instead!

Going forward. Squeeze with your calves and allow with the reins. Release the leg pressure as soon as the horse reacts.

Stopping and slowing down. Horses are trained to respond to the voice command "Whoa," and the rider should lift the hand holding the reins up and toward her stomach. Sit up and press down with your seat bones.

Turning. Look in the direction you want to go and move your rein hand in that direction. Shift your weight over to that side to encourage the horse to move underneath you. Use your outside leg to give a clearer command to the horse and keep the impulsion.

THE WALK

The Western-trained horse should walk freely with long open strides that are not hindered by the restrictive rein contact of English riding. The rider should relax and go with the movement of the horse, with their legs hanging freely using a long length of stirrup.

THE JOG

The jog is the Western equivalent of a trot. It is a very comfortable, slow gait that is ridden seated. This can be accelerated into a trot, and because it is more difficult to rise to the trot in a Western saddle, it is possible to hold a raised position, slightly out of the saddle, with your weight pushing down into the stirrups. You are almost standing so that the bumpy movement will not be felt.

THE LOPE

This is similar to a slow, collected canter but is less elevated. The aids are similar to those used for a canter: you aim to flex the horse's nose to the inside with your rein and squeeze with the outside leg behind the cinch. Keep your body and legs relaxed and follow the movement.

TIP Whether riding English or Western style, the goal is that the rider's aids should be so subtle that an onlooker only sees the horse's response, not the rider's cues.

◀ **Even if you ride purely** *for fun at home or on trails, you could try entering some competitions to show off your equitation skills. This is a Western-style walk.*

◣ **In neck reining,** *the horse moves away from the slight weight of the rein that he feels on his neck, not through direct bit contact.*

▼ **"Whoa!" Use your voice** *to stop as you bring the rein in close to your belly button and sink deep into the saddle. Release your hand forward again when the horse responds.*

Western riding disciplines

If you enjoy the Western style of riding and like a challenge, why not enter a Western competition? You might like to try one of the following disciplines. Reining is now included as an Olympic equestrian sport, so aim high!

WESTERN HORSEMANSHIP

Western Horsemanship judges your equitation skills, so your position in the saddle and correct use of aids is important. Riders are asked to follow a set pattern of maneuvers individually at walk, trot, and lope, so accuracy is very important. A shortlist of finalists then ride as a group for the final placings to be decided.

WESTERN PLEASURE

A Western Pleasure class tests the ability of a horse and rider to change gaits and leads at predetermined points around the course in walk, jog, and lope. Smoothness

▲ **A sliding stop** *during a reining competition brings the horse to a sharp halt from canter in a cloud of dust.*

and accuracy of movements are essential because points are awarded for successfully changing gait precisely between the middle of a pair of cones.

REINING

Reining demonstrates the speed, obedience, and versatility of a good ranch horse. Patterns are included to test style and responsiveness: small controlled circles, large fast circles, flying lead changes, sliding stops, and rollbacks, plus amazing 360 degree spins. There are classes with set

◀ **The latest fashion trend** *is important to competitive Western Pleasure riders.*
▶ **Good handling** *and presentation skills are vital in a Showmanship class.*

TIP If your horse has bridling and bit problems, then a change to the Western style of riding in a bosal hackamore could give him a new career.

each competitor is asked to walk their horse through a series of patterns and maneuvers.

BARREL RACING

Barrel racing is becoming increasingly popular because it requires very few props for training – just a horse and three oil drums! The idea is to race around the barrels in a cloverleaf pattern as fast as possible, which requires amazing acceleration and the ability to turn as tightly as possible around each barrel. Each run is timed, and competition is fierce.

▲ **Barrel racing is done** *at high speed – racing against the clock and making tight turns around the barrels.*

patterns and also freestyle, which can be performed to music.

SHOWMANSHIP

Showmanship is an excellent class if you get nervous riding in front of a judge. Instead, you lead your horse into the ring and stand him up for the judge to inspect the grooming and presentation of the horse. Your horse handling skills are also assessed as

TRAIL

A trail class is designed to test your ability to negotiate the obstacles you may encounter out on a trail. Obstacles such as gates, logs, and poles are set up to mimic hazards you may have to pass by, over, or reverse through. Scoring takes into account the accuracy of the riding, and the ease and willingness of the horse through the obstacles.

◀ **Trail riding obstacles,** *such as this bridge, are set up to mimic hazards found on a trail.*

TURNING AND BENDING

In a trot everything is happening faster, so you need to give your horse clear aids in time to make the turns at the appropriate markers. You are aiming for flowing, not jerky, changes of direction and circles without edges.

To trot a large circle covering one end of the arena (a 60 ft/20 m circle), you should touch the track on each side of the arena and cut through the "imaginary" marker at X in the center. A 33 ft (10 m) circle leaves the track on the side of the arena, touches the center line, and then curves back onto the original track. Always practice circles on both reins to keep your horse supple.

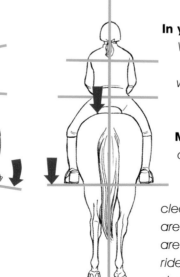

▲ Avoid motorbiking!
Keep your inside hand high if your horse has a tendency to lean in when going around corners.

Here are the top tips on making bends and circles:
- Look ahead in the direction you want to go.
- Sit up straight.
- Don't just move your horse's head, bend his whole body around your leg like a banana.

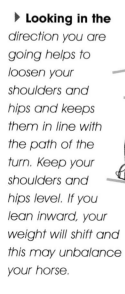

▶ Looking in the
direction you are going helps to loosen your shoulders and hips and keeps them in line with the path of the turn. Keep your shoulders and hips level. If you lean inward, your weight will shift and this may unbalance your horse.

1
In your mind's eye
Visualize the line of the turn you want to achieve.

Mind reading
does not come easily to a horse, so make your signals clear and logical. There are some horsess who are better than their riders at learning dressage tests though!

2
In control
Rest your outside leg behind the girth to stop his quarters from swinging out, and control your speed with the outside rein.

Do not try to jerk your horse around with a harsh pull on one rein.

▸ **Cones, buckets, and barrels** *are great for perfecting your bending. Why not have a bending race with your friends?*

A SERPENTINE

A serpentine is a snake-shaped figure taking you from one side of the school to the other in a series of three loops. You can start this at either A or C and you should finish at the other end of the school, facing in the opposite direction. The aim is to make each of the half-circles a good shape, all touching the edge of the arena and linked by straight lines going across three-quarters of the arena. It may help to place markers just off the track to help you assess distances and stop you from falling in off the track.

4
Use the reins
Bend his head to the inside and allow with your outside rein.

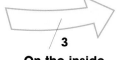

3
On the inside
Your inside leg should squeeze on the girth to maintain the trot.

A

F K

B E

M H

START

C

Mastering the rein-back

THE REIN-BACK

The rein-back is a very useful movement, but it is harder to achieve than it looks. Here's how to ride the rein-back.

- **Begin** with a good square halt. Hold the reins with an equal light contact, and keep your legs still and your seat, hips, and back soft. Do not slump in the saddle.
- **Now lighten** your seat, tipping forward very slightly so there is less weight in the saddle. This helps to allow room for your horse's back to arch as he performs the movement.

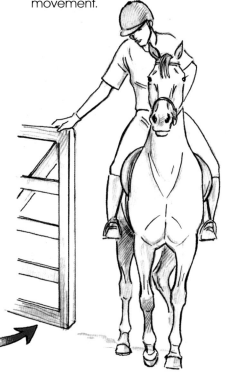

- **Contain** the forward movement with your hands as you apply your legs slightly behind the girth. Your horse may be slightly confused because you are asking him to go forward but not letting him.
- **Think** backward.
- **Squeeze** each rein alternately in time with the horse's backward steps.
- **You may need** to adjust his straightness by correcting him with one leg behind the girth if his quarters try to swing out.

◀ **Skills such as the rein-back** are more than just training exercises. They equip you to tackle obstacles you meet on a ride.

1
Polework challenge
Poles on the ground will assist in keeping your horse straight. This exercise is used as a test in Le Trec, so you will soon be an expert! Keep central and walk forward through the poles.

Keep central between the poles.

2
Halt. Head up, heels down
When your horse's front hooves clear the corridor of poles, halt and wait for three seconds.

TIP It may help your horse if you actually say the word "back" as you are asking him to go backwards, or get someone to apply pressure to his chest to start him off.

GOALS

Preparation for a show or dressage test. Level of difficulty (3).

Trot a figure eight then come up the center line and halt at X. Rein-back for 4 steps.

Halt. Walk forward for 8 steps. Halt and practice saluting a judge.

3
Relax and rein-back

Soften your seat and ask your horse to rein-back right through the channel of poles. Use your legs behind the girth to stop him from going crooked and knocking a pole. Halt.

4
Finish with focus

Look ahead and walk actively forward through the poles onto the track.

Did You Know?

In rein-back your horse's feet move in diagonal formation, for example, off-hind, near-fore, then near-hind followed by off-fore.

The arena

Even if you do not have the benefit of a surfaced manège or fenced arena, it is useful to mark out the area you use to practice your riding skills in the same way as a dressage arena. This helps to give you clear, identified points at which to change gait or direction and will assist with productive schooling and give your teacher a clear means of communicating instructions to you. You will also be able to practice a dressage test before being judged at a competition.

The arena has a number of markers arranged around the outside, each bearing a letter (see diagram). It helps to think of a memorable sentence to remind you of the order of the arena markers. For the letters of a large arena, clockwise from point A, you can use a phrase such as "All Kind Elephants Have Cute Mothers, Big Fathers." For the letters in an counter-clockwise direction from A, how about "A Fine Bay Mare Can Hardly Ever Kick?"

To remember the markers down the center line, try to memorize this little phrase: A – D – X – G – C "All Daddies X (kiss) Grannies Carefully!"

TIP: If you are asked, for example, to trot at M, this means that when your horse's shoulder is level with the marker you should be in trot, so you may have to give your aids a stride or two beforehand.

GOAL: Try riding each of these figures, keeping the lines straight and accurate to the markers and the circles round and not egg-shaped.

▶ **Letters around the arena** *give precise points where you can change gait or direction for more productive schooling or when practicing for a dressage test.*

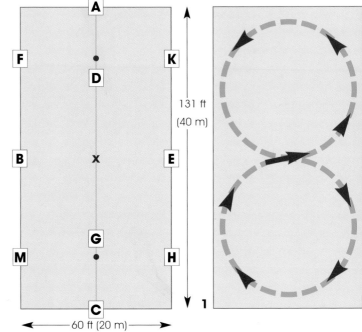

TIP Keep your inside hand high and your inside leg strongly on the girth if your horse keeps falling in on the circles (i.e., he is not keeping out to the track or the markers).

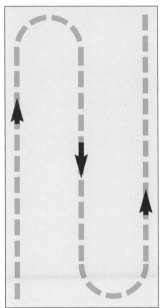

2

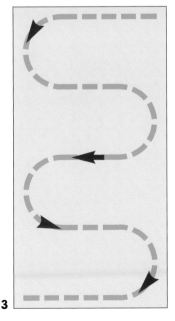

3

4

▲ **Ride accurately to each marker,** *especially if you are in a group lesson. Don't let your horse play "follow the leader," tagging behind the horse in front without thinking.*

◄ **Make schooling fun** *by riding several different configurations around the arena. Plan exactly what you are going to do and perfect it before moving on to the next exercise. Ride each pattern in both directions to keep your horse supple.*

IMPROVING BALANCE AND IMPULSION

When you start riding, the movements that you experience can feel very unnatural because you are using different muscles and having to cope with the movement of the horse. Here are some exercises to help improve your sense of balance and make you feel more secure in the saddle.

RIDING WITHOUT REINS

It is important not to hang on the reins when you ride in order to stabilize yourself or you will jab the horse in his mouth and make him sore. Learning to think more about your balance and leg aids will help you to improve your riding. For this reason, riding without holding the reins is a very useful exercise. However, it would be dangerous to simply drop the reins for two reasons:

1. Tie your reins in a knot near the buckle to shorten them so they don't dangle down. You can still grab them in front of the knot if needed.
2. Ask you horse or pony to walk or trot on.
3. Be aware of where your hands are – have they shot upward or are they still in the correct place as if you are still holding on to the imaginary reins?
4. If you feel unstable, hold on to the pommel of the saddle until you rebalance yourself.
5. Try making turns with your horse just by turning your shoulders and using your outside leg back behind the girth to direct him.
6. When you want to slow down, say "Whoa," press down with your seat, and be sure to pick up the reins again if your horse does not decelerate.

▲ **Tie a knot** in your reins before you begin.

- They could hang down and get caught up or trodden on by the horse.
- Your horse could sense he is loose and run off with you on his back.

Therefore, to be safe, make sure you are in a confined space and begin by just walking around the arena, or ask someone either to lead you or put your horse on a longe line so they can prevent him from running off.

▲ **Balance is the key** to a secure seat, especially when jumping. An inexperienced rider could jab the horse in the mouth or be unseated.

▲ **Sit tall and stretch** your legs down because you may be gripping with your knees to compensate. Your helper can keep an eye on your position.

◀ **Look at me!** You will soon be confident and know that you don't rely on your reins to stay balanced.

◀◀ **Hold the pommel** if you feel unstable, but don't look down.

Riding without stirrups

Using stirrups gives you extra security because you can push against them to maintain your balance, especially if a horse shies without warning. They also assist you in rising trot and when jumping because you can stand up in them to lift your weight out of the saddle (*below*).

The benefits of practicing riding without stirrups are that you will find you become more aware of the movement of the horse. Often your position will improve because your legs will naturally hang down long, without being forced into a specific shape so that they can slide into the stirrups.

1. Take your feet out of your stirrups and cross the stirrups over the horse's withers to prevent them from knocking the horse's sides or getting caught up in anything.
2. If you allow your leg to hang down, you will find that you are sitting more deeply in the saddle.
3. Still try to keep your heels down and your toes facing forward.
4. Sit up tall and keep your eyes looking up and ahead of you.
5. Ask your horse to walk or trot on. If the trot is bouncy, slow him down a little and you will find it easier.
6. If you feel unstable, take your reins in one hand and hold the pommel of the saddle with the other.
7. Try not to grip with your knees because this will lift you out of the saddle and make your lower legs rigid. By keeping your thighs in contact with the saddle, you can sit back or roll forward on them to adjust your weight in the saddle

▲ **Bareback riding** *puts you in tune with the horse's movements. Without stirrups you need good balance!*

while still keeping your lower legs free to give the aids. After a bit of practice, you will soon find that you can still do rising trot and even canter and jump without stirrups!

WARNING: It is all too easy to break a stirrup leather by catching it on a gatepost, or to lose a stirrup if your horse bucks underneath you. For this reason, it makes a lot of sense to learn to ride without them. Being able to ride without stirrups could be crucial to your becoming a safe rider.

TIP Shake your legs out so you know they are not tense or gripping. Really feel your weight drop into your seat bones.

◀ **Cross over your stirrups** *so they lie flat in front of the saddle. Cross the right one over first and then the left one. Stirrups left dangling would knock against the horse and your ankle uncomfortably.*

◥ **Until you are confident,** *get a lead so you can forget about steering and hold the pommel of the saddle.*

▼ **Perfection without stirrups!** *As she goes over the jump, this rider is pivoting on her knees to get her weight out of the saddle and is balanced enough not to lean on her reins.*

Mounted exercises for the rider

Being fit and flexible will help greatly with your riding. If you are able to stay in good balance with the horse and be light in the saddle, it will help you to become a responsive rider. If you get tired and sit heavily "like a sack of potatoes" bumping around and unbalancing your horse, it won't be comfortable for either of you.

Here are some exercises to improve your coordination and balance in the saddle.

- Around the world *(right)*
- Touching toes *(below)*
- Torso twists *(opposite page, lower left)*
- Sunbathing/stargazing *(below right)*

▲ **Touch your right toe** *with your left hand, then left toe with your right hand.*

▶ **Stargazing/sunbathing** *is fun, but make sure someone holds your horse!*

TIP If you feel tense when on horseback, try circling each shoulder back in turn, and then together, to loosen and relax you.

SUPPLING EXERCISES FOR THE HORSE

Horses can get stiff too, and if you have a spare few minutes before you ride, loosen up your horse with a few of these exercises.

- Carrot stretch sideways *(below)*
- Carrot stretch between forelegs *(bottom left)*
- Foreleg stretch *(bottom right)*

▲ **Around the world** *involves doing scissors around your horse so you face forward, sideways, backward, sideways, and finally end up in your starting position.*

◀ **To twist your torso,** *swing from side to side with your arms extended.*

▲ **Stretching each foreleg** *forward gently smoothes out creases under the girth and is good practice for when the farrier needs to do it.*

The importance of poles

Going around and around an arena can become tedious for both horse and rider. But quite often an obstacle or two are all that are needed to create some interest and renewed energy in a schooling session. Using trotting poles set out on the ground requires the horse/rider combination to be aware of the length of their striding in order to float over the poles rather than knocking them. It also exaggerates the elevation of the paces and improves self-carriage and flexibility in the horse. It is your first step to learning how to jump too.

Start with a single pole at walk (especially if your horse is young or easily spooked), and be aware of how the horse looks at the pole on approach and negotiates it, one leg at a time, hopefully without striking it.

Your instructor can then set out three or four poles in a line at the correct distance to suit your horse's striding (or an average distance if there are several horses taking part on the ride). This is usually around 3 to 4 ft (1 to 1.2 m) apart for an averagely sized horse.

▲ **The approach is very important.** *Aim straight for the center of each pole and keep an active, rhythmic pace.*

To ride the line of poles:

- Keep your horse/pony straight – ride for the center of each pole.
- Look up at all times, don't look down – you will be able to feel and hear if your horse does knock a pole!
- Stay in a rhythmical, active walk or trot – pushing on with your legs if your horse hesitates or steadying with the hands and seat if the horse tries to rush.
- Allow with the rein contact when your horse needs to stretch out and lengthen his stride.

Ride over the line of poles in both directions until you float over them without that dreaded "clonk" of hitting a pole – practice makes perfect!

▲ **Both horse and rider** can find schooling work boring. *Setting up some poles will give you both renewed interest.*

TIP As you go over each pole, lift your seat slightly out of the saddle to enable the horse to raise his back.

▲ **You can continue** in rising trot. You should feel the added elevation as your horse clears each pole.

▲ **Ride actively out** of the line of poles – don't just relax afterwards, but imagine you are riding to another obstacle.

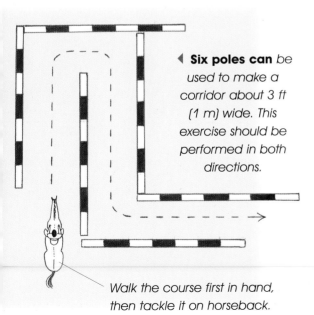

◀ **Six poles can** be used to make a corridor about 3 ft (1 m) wide. This exercise should be performed in both directions.

Walk the course first in hand, then tackle it on horseback.

▲ **This rider has adopted** a slightly forward seat to allow her horse to really extend over the single pole.

Poles in different configurations

RAISED POLES

Try lifting a couple of the poles slightly off the ground on stands and feel the extra elevation of your horse's legs that becomes necessary in order to clear the poles. Because he has to work harder with his hind legs and back, this helps with engagement of the hindquarters. It is very useful for horses that tend to slob around "on the forehand" and usually feel heavy in the reins. Bear in mind that an elderly or arthritic horse may find raised poles challenging due to the extra flexion required. Any reluctance or excessive knocking of poles or audible joint clicking should be examined before continuing with these exercises.

Warning: Keep raised poles well spaced apart when in trot, or your horse may try to jump them all at once!

POLES IN A FAN

Set out poles in a corner of the arena, fanning them out to make an arc. Because they are narrower on the inside than the outside, you can decide where to place the horse in order to make him shorten and elevate or reach out and lengthen his stride.

CANTER POLES

Cantering over poles helps to create a balanced rhythmical canter and assists with both collection and impulsion (control and power).

These need to be spaced further apart than with the trotting poles – about 11 to 12 ft (3.3 to 3.6 m) for a horse but closer for a pony.

Bear in mind you are traveling much faster and the poles come up very quickly, without much time for adjustment. So it is essential to try to get the striding pattern right as you approach the first pole.

▲ **Alternate the raised side** of the poles or your horse is likely to drift to the low end rather than staying central. Look ahead and keep him straight with your legs.

▲ **Poles positioned in a fan** give you the opportunity to really stretch your horse over the wide outside arc.

TIP Ordinary jump poles can be turned into great learning devices, showing the horse a new way of moving and becoming more elastic – all it takes is imagination!

▲ **This horse is having to think** *about where he positions each leg, and you can see how he has to reach with his hind leg to avoid touching the pole.*

▲ **A good straight exit,** *but the rider needs to keep riding strongly forward after clearing the final pole to maintain the activity that she has just created.*

▲ **Horse and rider** *have to be accurate when riding the tight inside arc but still need to maintain impulsion.*

▲ **Using canter poles** *as part of your schooling is a good way to keep an exuberant horse balanced and focused.*

Understanding impulsion and collection

IMPULSION

Impulsion is the pushing power of the horse to create forward or upward movement. A horse needs adequate impulsion to enable him to move with active paces and in order to have the power to clear a jump. Some horses are naturally more forward-going due to their conformation or their breeding, while other horses are sluggish and require a lot of leg and seat aids to encourage them. A fit horse will have more impulsion than an overweight or unfit animal – however much "rocket fuel" feed you give him!

▶ **Horses carry** *60 percent of the weight on their forelegs and need schooling to bring the center of gravity back.*

This rider is just a passenger and is not creating energy.

A loose rein allows an unschooled horse to let all the energy "out the front door."

The energy is harnessed between leg and hand so the horse steps further underneath himself. The center of gravity has moved back.

COLLECTION

You may hear your instructor asking you to "collect" your horse and make him "engage" his hindquarters. Physically, this means the horse will be compressing the length of his body, his hind legs will be reaching farther forward under him, while his neck will be raised and arched with his face perpendicular to the ground. The hind legs create the power and the rein contact holds it in check, harnessing the power rather than allowing the horse forward at a more hurried pace. The result is that if

you collect your horse effectively, his paces will be more elevated – they may feel slower and more bouncy to sit to.

Combining impulsion with collection (i.e., driving the horse forward with your legs into the rein contact) will create a horse that is "on the bit." If your horse tends to ride "flat" with his nose poking out or runs along in trot rather than doing a nice transition into canter, then you need to practice your impulsion and collection skills.

TIP It is well worth having a lesson from a dressage schoolmaster. It is such a thrill finally to "get it" when the horse responds perfectly to the correct aids.

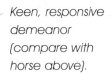

◄ **A horse that feels heavy** is "on the forehand." More impulsion is needed.

▶ **The head should be carried** just ahead of the vertical, not poking out or overbent inward.

Rider sits quietly and gives accurate aids.

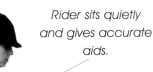

Keen, responsive demeanor (compare with horse above).

Horse is reaching down into the rein contact but still feels light.

Expressive paces because the horse is working actively from behind.

◄ **Ask someone to video** you riding so you can review your riding prowess with your instructor and criticize or praise the result!

RIDING IN PAIRS AND GROUPS

Practicing your riding with friends is good fun but requires skill to prevent your horses from colliding and so that you all keep in pace with each other.

ETIQUETTE

- If you pass in opposite directions on the track, you should pass left shoulder to left shoulder (*below*).
- Do not get too close to the horse in front or your horse might get kicked. Aim to allow a distance of about a full horse's length between each animal.

You can ask your instructor if you can practice riding in pairs, trying to keep precisely in line so that each rider is parallel. The rider on the outside will have to ask his/her horse to step out more on the corners because they will be taking a wider line. The rider on the inside may have to hold the horse back a little.

There are national competitions for pairs and also quadrilles (which means a team of four). Most teams put on a really theatrical performance and have music tracks specially mixed to match the horse's paces and wear themed costumes.

GOAL: Make up your own pairs dressage routine, including a figure eight and circles on both reins. Start by coming down the center line together at A, but include an element where you split off and go in opposing directions before pairing up again. Remember to finish by saluting at X.

You can make your schooling sessions a lot more fun by playing music to which you ride. Pick music with a rhythmical beat, and try to keep your horse in time with the beat. Horses can feel uplifted and inspired by music just as we can; however, it may take a little time before you work out his favorite style!

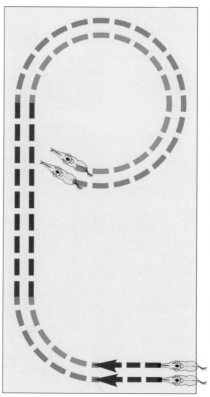

- - - — *Longer strides*
- - - — *Shorter strides*
- - - — *Matching stride*

◄ **When approaching the corners,** *the outside horse needs to extend and the inside horse shorten in order to keep together. The larger or longer striding horse should take the outside track to make this easier.*

► **Keep your shoulders** *in line with one another and try to regulate the pace so the striding pattern is identical, like this.*

TIP These exercises are easier when ridden at rising trot. You can regulate the speed by rising faster or slower.

◀ **When riding in single file,** *don't let your horse hang onto the rear of the horse in front. Keep a distance of about a horse's length between you.*

▼ **Look across the arena** *and regulate your speed so that you and your pair reach the center line and turn in precisely together.*

Riding out safely

Some of the most pleasurable times that you will spend with your horse or pony are likely to be when you are hacking out or trail riding together. Whether it is just the two of you sharing an excursion and bonding through your shared adventures, or if you are out on a group ride with friends, it pays to be aware of road sense, countryside rules, and good horse etiquette (manners).

BE SEEN

- High-visibility clothing or horsewear is the first step to safety on the roads because the drivers of cars and trucks will see you sooner, giving them valuable seconds to slow down as they approach you.
- Always carry a cell phone. You may encounter problems miles from home, so a phone is **essential**.
- Tell someone at the stable the route you are taking. Should you need their help, at least they will know which direction to go in.
- If you are riding with friends and chatting, pay attention to other road users and ride in single file if someone is trying to pass you.
- Always acknowledge thoughtful drivers – a smile and a thank you **does** make a real difference to how they will react to the next horse rider they meet.
- If you go through a gate, make sure that you close it afterwards.
- If you go onto a grassy area, be vigilant as there may be rubbish hidden there, or holes or ditches into which your horse could step and injure himself.

HIGHWAY CODE FOR HORSE RIDERS

1. Quick wave = *Thank you*
2. Palm facing the oncoming traffic or traffic behind = *Stop please*
3. Outstretched arm to the right = *Turning right*
4. Outstretched arm to the left = *Turning left*
5. Outstretched arm with small circling wrist motion = *It is safe for you to pass*
6. Raising and lowering an outstretched arm = *Slow down please*

▲ **Hi-vis clothing** *is a life-saver. Car drivers will see you earlier, and it gives them valuable seconds in which to slow down.*

▼ **When riding alone,** *tell someone your route and expected time of return and always take a cell phone. Never go out late or you may find yourself short of daylight.*

◀ **When riding in company** *it can be easy to get distracted while chatting. Keep an eye out for holes and hazards and also recognizable landmarks that you can recall if you lose your way.*

STARTING JUMPING

By now you are well on the way to becoming a proficient and confident rider. Are you ready for the next challenge – jumping? Learning to jump is fun and asks questions of both horse and rider. It is not for the faint-hearted!

BEFORE YOU START

- In addition to your normal essential riding gear (helmut and suitable footwear), I would suggest that you wear a body protector.
- A neck strap on the horse gives you something to clasp for stability as you go over the jump, and it stops you from hanging on the reins and hurting the horse's mouth.
- Shorten your stirrups by a couple of holes – this will help you to lift your weight forward and out of the saddle.

You can begin your jumping lessons by extending your pole work to include a low jump instead of the final pole. Trotting over the poles will keep the horse steady, enabling you to concentrate on your position. It's quite likely that the horse or pony will land in a canter after the jump, so hold onto a chunk of mane or a neck strap if you are at all unsteady.

If you want to jump higher, your instructor will probably suggest you approach the fence in canter to make it easier for the horse to propel himself up and over the fence. It is also more comfortable for you – a horse is more likely to cat-leap a larger fence when working in trot.

◄ **A body protector** will cushion you in the unfortunate event that you hit the floor or land on top of a jump after a refusal.

▶ **Don't hang onto the reins** for balance – hold the neck strap for extra stability in the air.

TIP If your horse is not keen on jumping or wary of a particular obstacle, follow behind another horse to give him confidence.

◀◀ **Shorten your stirrups** by a couple of holes. This will help you secure your forward position as the horse moves beneath you.

◀ **Your pole work** will pay dividends because poles can be used to put the horse on the right stride for a perfect takeoff.

Look ahead in the direction that you want to go.

Flatten your back and bring your chest down over the neck.

Pivot from your hips and knees to lift your seat out of the saddle.

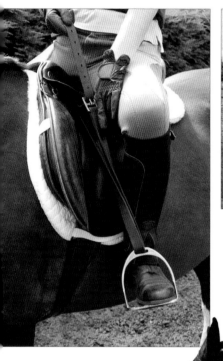

▶ **This is the jumping position.** *Think of squashing down rather than throwing yourself forward or upward. It is only your hands that need to move up the neck.*

Allow your hands forward as the horse stretches over the fence.

Keep your lower leg still, with all your weight taken in the stirrups.

Starting jumping

It helps to think of jumping as a movement that happens in four stages:

1 THE APPROACH
- Look at the jump.
- Stay in an active but rounded trot or canter.
- Aim for the center of the fence.
- Sit deep a couple of strides beforehand.
- Check with the reins or encourage with the legs to keep the horse balanced.

2 THE TAKE OFF
- As the horse lifts his forelegs off the ground, transfer your weight into your stirrups.
- Take up the forward seat.
- Move your hands farther up your horse's neck to allow him more rein.

3 MIDAIR
- Look ahead and toward the next jump if you are jumping a course.
- Start to unfurl your forward position to rebalance yourself in readiness for the landing.

4 LANDING
- Sit up but be sure not to jab the horse in the mouth.
- Put your legs on to help pick the horse up and traveling forward.
- Collect the rein contact and steer the horse to the next fence.

TIP: It is possible to influence the horse's canter lead in midair so that you will be on the correct leg on landing. This is very useful if you have to turn after a jump because the horse will be more balanced and you won't have to make him switch legs or take him back to trot to get him around a tight corner. Give the aids – outside leg, inside hand – as you go over the fence so the horse will know which way he has to turn on landing. This is especially useful in a competitive jump-off!

TIP If you find that you keep losing your stirrups, you are probably gripping with your knees because your stirrups are too long, so shorten the leathers by a couple of holes.

▶ **Pivot at the knee** and hip, and put your weight onto the ball of your foot.

Rider has gotten left behind, hindering the horse.

Hands fixed restricting the horse.

Body too upright.

Too much daylight between bottom and saddle.

Progressing with jumping

As you increase in confidence with your jumping, you may want to try taking part in some basic competitions. Many shows run jumping courses where every competitor will get a ribbon for jumping the course with no faults. Then there are classes in which competitors are grouped according to the age of the rider or the height of their horse or pony. If more than one rider jumps the course clear, then there is a Jump Off, which means riders try to go around a shorter (but usually higher) course while they are being timed, and the fastest clear round (or the one with the fewest faults if no one goes clear) wins the class.

A **"fault"** is the term for clocking up penalties for mistakes during a round, such as:
* Missing a jump or jumping the wrong course.
* Knocking down a pole.
* Refusing or running out at a fence.

These faults and ways of helping to prevent or overcome them are explained below.

▲ **If your horse runs out** at a fence, don't be too quick to blame him – were **you** fully committed to the jump?

RUNNING OUT

If a horse or pony runs out to one side, he is trying to take the easy option by avoiding the fence completely. It is up to you to show that you are committed to jumping it and are determined to make sure that he will too!

Build fences that look inviting and that don't have easy escape routes. Cross poles and fences with wide wings are ideal—they encourage the horse to aim for the center. For added assistance, rest poles on either side of the fence to channel the horse into the jump.

Keep your reins short on the approach, and keep your legs on the horse's sides to drive him forward. Be ready to adjust the pressure at the split second that you feel him beginning to veer off course.

JUMPING THE WRONG COURSE

You are normally allowed to walk the course before the class starts. This literally means walking around on foot, which enables you to think about the approach to each jump, when you will need to ask your horse to change leg at canter, and the striding pattern between any combination fences. Each fence or combination obstacle is numbered.

It is important to memorize the course in your mind and be confident that you will not lose your way – if you do, or miss a fence, or jump one in the wrong direction, it is very likely that you will be eliminated from the class (which means disqualification). It is usual in a jump-off competition for a notice board to be put up with a list of the numbers of the jumps being used in the shortened course displayed in order to show you the route. This time, for instance, you may have to jump fence 1 and then 6a and 6b, and then come back to number 2. Again, a good memory is required, as well as speed and jumping ability.

TIP   Set up three jumps together to make a U-shape. You don't need many jump stands, and you have scope to jump the fences in many different ways.

▲ **Guiding poles** *can be easily used to channel the horse into the jump.*

▶ **Look, no hands!** *As your confidence grows, try tying a knot in your reins and keeping in perfect balance over the fence.*

◀◀ **Don't overface your horse** – *lower the fences if he is losing confidence and knocking or refusing them.*

◀ **If you have the opportunity,** *show your horse as many "scary" fences and bright fillers as you can. You will have less chance of a spook or refusal in the show ring.*

Knocking down a pole

It is unfortunate if you horse just touches a pole and it falls. He may just have gotten a little too close to the fence or not tucked his forelegs underneath enough or even caught the rail with a hind hoof. It's disappointing, and you normally incur four faults per fence you knock down, but do not reprimand your horse. He has at least attempted the jump and perhaps the striding was wrong or he was simply getting tired, so work on his general fitness and try to improve your own accuracy when riding the course.

REFUSALS

A horse that refuses or runs out at the side of a fence has decided he does not want to jump it! You may have "overfaced" him (attempted a jump too high or complicated for the horse's experience), or he may just be lazy and taking the easy route. You normally get four faults for the first refusal, eight for the second, and elimination for the third disobedience in show jumping. Hesitation, circling, or stepping back can be counted as disobedience, and taking the wrong course leads to immediate elimination. Check the rules for your class.

It is essential to be committed yourself to jumping the fence – any nerves or anxiety that you are feeling will be transmitted to the horse. Keep your reins short and your legs on, channeling him into the center of the fence. If your horse has a tendency to refuse, grab a chunk of mane or use a neck strap for added stability to avoid flying over his shoulder if he does stop suddenly.

Take care not to cross your own path between obstacles during the course of a round because this can also be counted as a refusal in a show jumping arena.

▲ **The value of a body protector** *cannot be overstated, especially because poles don't make for a soft landing!*

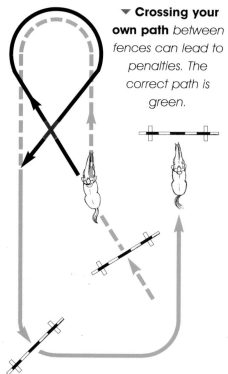

▼ **Crossing your own path** *between fences can lead to penalties. The correct path is green.*

TIP If you jump your horse over slightly higher fences in the warmup arena, he should be more on his toes to clear the lower fences in the ring.

▲ **A rushing horse** can be steadied by leg yielding across the diagonal and only allowing one canter stride before the next fence.

▲ **Build courses that require** a the horse to do a "double take." It will keep him focused.

▲ **Falls do happen,** and every horse and rider has an off day. Don't despair, keep practicing!

◀ **Never chastise a horse** for knocking a pole. He has jumped keenly for you and the knock will have shown him he needs to jump higher.

Types of fences

SHOW JUMPS

These are normally set up in a fenced arena or paddock and numbered to show the order and direction in which you should tackle the fences. The poles normally sit on cups and can be knocked down quite easily if touched by the horse's hoof or leg.

- Upright
- Spread
- Double
- Treble
- Oxer
- Wall
- Combination

A vertical jump consists of poles set above each other with no spread, or width, to jump.

WORKING HUNTER FENCES

They are based on show jumps, but these fences look rustic, using natural wood poles, greenery, and brush and often include an obstacle, such as a stile, to imitate what you may need to jump while out hunting.

CROSS-COUNTRY FENCES

These can be spread over several miles of a course, with plenty of canters or gallops between each obstacle. A flag on each corner of the jump denotes the direction in which it should be taken – red on the left and white on the right. The jumps are usually permanently constructed (the poles don't fall down if knocked) and are therefore unforgiving if a horse knocks them. Fortunately, horses tend to really enjoy cross-country, so even a horse that can be stuffy and slow in the show ring may excel at cross-country!

- Stile
- Ditch
- Oxer
- Water complex

TIP: Visit a nationally renowned event and gain some inspiration from watching the professionals ride. You will be amazed at the immense size of the fences that they can jump.

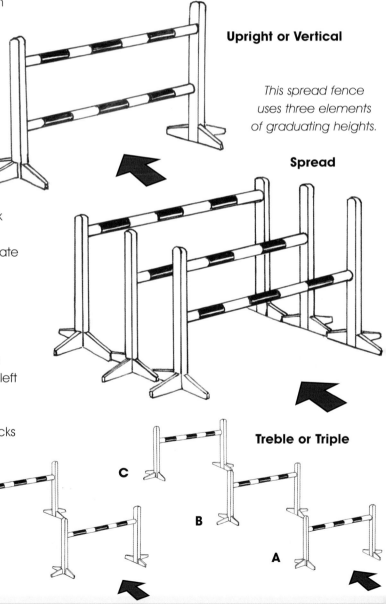

Upright or Vertical

This spread fence uses three elements of graduating heights.

Spread

Treble or Triple

C

B

A

Double

TIP Large equestrian centers usually have superb equipment. Enter their classes to let your horse experience different jumps.

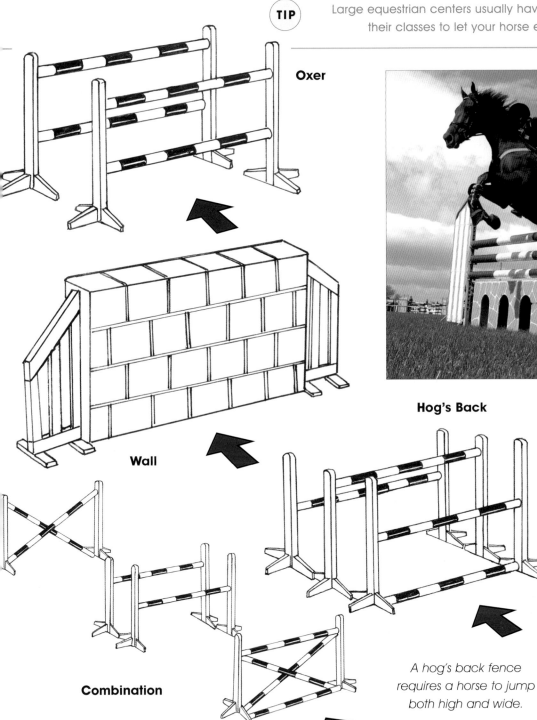

Oxer

Wall

Combination

Hog's Back

▲ **Watch at large shows** *for inspiration, then make your dream a reality!*

▲ **Use colored tape** *or pole sleeves over lengths of drainpipe to make, inexpensive poles.*

A hog's back fence requires a horse to jump both high and wide.

DRESSAGE

LEARNING A DRESSAGE TEST

Dressage may not initially seem as exhilarating as jumping or riding across country, but this competition is all about achieving a perfect partnership with your horse and displaying the beauty and athleticism that every horse possesses. You may feel daunted by competing in your first dressage test. Will you remember the test? Will your circles be round and your turns accurate?

This is what a dressage test sheet looks like –

Introductory Level, Test A (Walk-Trot)

1	A X	Enter working trot rising. Halt through medium walk. Salute – Proceed medium walk.	*Coefficient*
2	C	Track right medium walk.	
3	M	Working trot rising.	
4	B B	Circle right 66 ft (20 m), working trot rising. Straight ahead.	2
5	Between B & F	Medium walk.	
6	K-X-M M	Free walk. Medium walk.	2
7	C	Working trot rising.	
8	E E	Circle left 66 ft (20 m), working trot rising. Straight ahead.	2
9	A X	Down centerline. Halt through medium walk. Salute.	

Leave arena in free walk on long rein. Exit at A.

Collective Marks

Gaits (freedom and regularity).	**1**
Impulsion (desire to move forward, relaxation of the back).	**2**
Submission (attention and confidence; harmony, lightness, and ease of movement: acceptance of bit with nose slightly in front of vertical).	**2**
Rider's position of seat, correctness, and effect of the aids.	**3**

You need to remember the sequence of paces and the patterns you will be making. Usually, everything is repeated on both reins, so if you break the test down into sections it should be easier to remember.

- Go through the test in your mind.
- Draw it out on a piece of paper, over and over again.
- Pretend to ride the test on foot – you may feel self-conscious, but it really helps!
- Ask someone to stand on the side of the arena and prompt you if you ask for directions.

The test sheet breaks down the test into the individual movements. The judge will mark each movement out of 10, with 10 being excellent, 9 very good, 8 good, 7 fairly good, 6 satisfactory, 5 sufficient, 4 insufficient, 3 fairly bad, 2 bad, 1 very bad, and 0 being given if the movement was not executed at all. There will also be comments about the general impression produced by the rider and the obedience of the horse. You should be pleased if you get 7s on a test (as 10s are rarely given) and the judge will write (hopefully constructive) comments against each movement so you will be able to see how you need to improve next time.

▶ **While learning a test,** *it is useful to have a helper to shout out if you need prompting about the directions, rather than trying to read the course route map while riding.*

◀ **It really helps** to draw out your test on paper or even practice it on foot. You may feel a bit silly at first, but at least you are not likely to forget it!

▶ **Finish your test** by saluting the judge. Most judges do not get paid, so they certainly deserve polite respect.

▼ **Keep your cool** as you perform your test. Remember you are "showing off" just how good a partnership you and your horse have managed to create.

Progressing in dressage

As well as practicing being accurate in your upward and downward transitions in walk, trot, and canter, the gaits are further subdivided in more advanced dressage to display rhythm, suppleness, and obedience by collection and extension.

WALK

Medium walk – a natural stride length, but always showing a purposeful rhythm, not shuffling or lazy.

Extended walk – you need to ask your horse to stretch out and lengthen each stride so he over-tracks his hoofprints (without hurrying or breaking into trot).

Collected walk – ask your horse to shorten his strides, but be sure to keep the impulsion for an active walk or he will just slow down or get tense.

Free walk – the rein contact is released so the horse has total freedom to lower his head and stretch out. Again, it should be active but it allows the horse to relax any tension.

The hind legs should track up to the hoof prints of the forelegs.

TROT

Working trot – the natural striding that the horse would take when asked to trot. The hind legs should track up to the prints of the forelegs (*as above*).

Medium trot – slightly longer strides than working trot, but not faster.

Extended trot – the horse will reach out elegantly with his legs, and his whole frame should appear to lower and lengthen in outline.

Collected trot – you will ask the horse to shorten his strides bringing his hind legs underneath him and channeling that energy to elevate the pace rather than extending it forward.

CANTER

Again, there are four different gaits: working, medium, extended, and collected canter. It is a balanced, rhythmical "uphill" canter that is desired. This means the horse should not look as if he is simply running along with the rider supporting a heavy head by the reins, but instead that the three beats of canter are "springy," with a clear moment of suspension in midair. The horse should look as though he carries you with ease.

▲ **A superb sequence** *of extended canter showing the powerful engagement of the quarters propelling the stride.*

TIP Walk your horse long and low at the start of each schooling session before asking for an outline. It allows him to stretch and warm his muscles so his outline will not be tense or fixed.

🔺 **Compare these three variants** of trot: (left to right) a balanced working trot, an expressive extended trot, and an elevated collected trot.

◀ **Free walk** on a long rein (far left) and medium walk. The horse is active and listening but has a relaxed gait.

🔺 **You can see how** the rider herself is lifted as the horse's back lifts just before the moment of suspension.

🔺 **The extension of the leading leg** is nicely illustrated in this expressive canter. The relaxed tail shows a free back.

CHAPTER ELEVEN

The half-halt

This is the secret that unfortunately I was never taught when I first learned to ride, but which is the Holy Grail of becoming a good rider. The half-halt is a subtle signal to your mount that you will want him to do something in a couple of strides' time – for example, before a change of pace or to check him in order to make him more balanced and listening to you.

- Sit deep.
- Check with your outside hand momentarily to restrict the forward movement.
- Squeeze with both heels to keep the impulsion going.
- After you feel the horse comply, immediately allow him forward again.

This should have the effect of creating lightness on the forehand and elevation of the pace momentarily.

LEG YIELDING

Leg yielding asks the horse to step sideways while continuing in a forward direction. It is termed a lateral movement. The horse will appear almost straight when viewed from the front, but both forelegs and hind legs will cross to produce a sideways motion. It is a useful way to promote suppleness, balance, and responsiveness to leg aids. It can be done in walk and trot.

On the right rein, come up the center line of the school at A with the aim of reaching the outside track at H.

- Sit up tall with your weight centrally in the saddle.
- Keep your horse's neck flexed very slightly to the right (although you are traveling to the left!).
- Apply the right leg on the girth to push him over to the left.
- Hold your left leg behind the girth to stop his quarters from swinging out and simply turning in a circle.
- Squeeze with your legs at each stride, and maintain a flexible rein contact to keep him moving forward.
- When you reach the track at H, give your horse a pat!

As with all exercises, try it on both reins so your horse does not favor one direction.

▶ **For a half-halt,** *squeeze the horse on with your legs but raise and close your hands to block any forward acceleration, then release.*

▼ **This horse starts well** *in trot (1) but then rushes as he falls onto the forehand and leans on the bit (2). The rider performs a half-halt (3) and this brings the horse back to him and lightens him in his hand (4).*

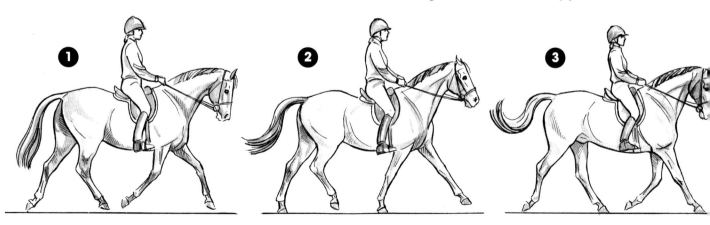

TIP Practice makes perfect. Go large around the arena in trot, and just before every corner practice the half-halt to balance and steady your horse.

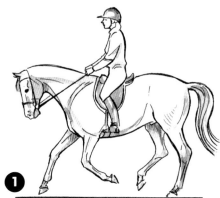

1

2

3

▲ **This horse is leaning** *on the bit in canter (**1**) so the rider uses a half-halt to rebalance him (**2**) and elevate the forehand (**3**).*

▶ **As he steps forward** *and sideways in leg yield, both hind and forelegs will cross as the horse moves laterally.*

4

▶▶ **Sit squarely** *and push the horse across from inside leg into the outside hand.*

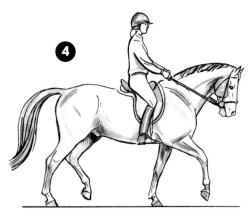

QUIZ – What sort of rider are you?

WHAT KIND OF RIDER AM I? WHERE SHOULD I GO FROM HERE?

Answer our quiz for some enlightening facts about yourself and to get ideas and inspiration for the future. Note the answer to each question that most nearly describes what you think, and then total up your letter scores and read the description that best applies to you.

1 What type of horses do you prefer to ride?

A Cobs, natives, and "Heinz 57" cross-breeds – safe, sensible, but fun is what I like.

B My own horse – he is perfect so I don't need to ride anything else.

C A handsome Warmblood or Quarterhorse – they're powerful and trainable, but have some common sense.

D Arabs, Thoroughbreds, Andalusians – these are stunningly beautiful horses, and I like the challenge of something a bit fiery too!

2 What do you like best about riding?

A I love the partnership with my horse – it's just an amazing feeling.

B Getting out into the countryside with my horse and friends too. Great fun!

C I enjoy the difference schooling can make – my horse and I have improved so much.

D Getting a buzz from a fast gallop or a competition – it just makes me want to ride more.

3 You enter a competition, but unfortunately things don't go your way and you finish second from last. How do you feel?

A How embarrassing! I never want to go through that again. I think I will stick to hacking.

B We had an off day. I must not let it affect me as I **know** we can do well. I will ask my instructor to do a mock test and see if she can identify where I may have gone wrong.

C It's so unfair, I think we did really well – the judging must have been fixed. I am not going to that show again.

D Oh well, it was an experience but a bit too much hanging around to bother again.

4 A friend offers you her fantastic, fit horse to take hunting or on an organized distance ride where you will be cantering in company. Do you …

A Dismiss it quickly – I have my own wonderful horse to ride that I feel comfortable on and I know we will have a fun time.

B Consider it seriously but worry that there will be too many out-of-control people on fast horses and you fear falling off, so you politely decline for safety reasons.

C Feel a bit apprehensive but agree as you know it will help your riding skills and level of experience.

D Imagine yourself riding the horse – the ride of your life. Shriek "Yes" and fill out the booking form for the event before she changes her mind!

5 What sort of riding clothes do you wear?

A The correct clothing for each discipline so I am neat and safe. Body protectors and hi-vis if needed too.

B Anything comfortable – jeans and boots. I often go for long rides.

C I like to look trendy – bright, designer brands that show I am really "horsey."

D Mainly casual. I don't really care on a day-to-day basis, but I do like to look the part when I am at a show when presentation counts.

6 If you went on a riding vacation, what would you prefer?

A Living in a gypsy caravan for a week being pulled by an adorable cob. Seeing the beautiful countryside with the gentle sound of clip-clop along the lanes. Bliss!

B Pretty green hilly scenery, and stopping off for a picnic every day.

C A week improving your cross-country skills at an equestrian center or learning something new like polo.

D Cantering along craggy, dusty paths on an Andalusian, Iberian, or Lusitano in Spain.

QUIZ – What sort of rider are you?

7 **Summer vacation has arrived. What do you look forward to most?**

A Spending more time with my horse – I don't care what I do.

B Going to horse summer camp – friends and horses, what more could I want!

C Being able to put in the hours to improve my riding and my horse's way of going. Schooling is such an art.

D Getting out to some competitions. I really want to have some fun and excitement with my horse.

ASSESSING YOUR ANSWERS

Mostly As

You love the companionship of your horse as much as the riding itself. You are sometimes overly cautious, which could limit your progress – but who cares! You ride simply because you enjoy being around horses, and that is just as fulfilling as winning a ribbon.

Possible horsey future: With your caring and methodical approach, perhaps you will be an equine therapist one day.

Mostly Bs

Well, you are so laid-back you are almost horizontal! You go with the flow and are equally happy to hack out with friends or to try something a bit daring. Everything you do is a good experience, and you treasure them all.

Possible horsey future: You get on well with people and aren't easily upset, so perhaps a groom or a riding instructor would be a good career.

Mostly Cs

You really are driven with your riding skills. You are willing to put in the time and effort needed to gain perfection – no one could ever say you weren't dedicated. Just remember, though, riding should be fun too and you do not want to alienate friends by being too critical and becoming a riding bore.

Possible horsey future: Perhaps you will be talent-spotted and given a sponsorship in your chosen sphere and put your competitiveness to good use.

Mostly Ds

Thrill-seeking cowboy/cowgirl! You don't really mind what you are doing or how well you are doing it as long as you get the buzz of adrenalin. You are always up for a challenge and aren't easily scared, but can be a bit reckless at times. Please consider safety issues but put your confidence to good use to inspire your not-so-brave friends to have a go at something new.

Possible horsey future: You would certainly get a buzz out of being a jockey riding racehorses, or perhaps would enjoy the cut and thrust of the polo field.

Glossary of Riding Terms

aids: The signals the rider uses to tell a horse what to do. Natural aids are the legs, seat, hands, and voice. Artificial aids are whips, spurs, and gadgets.

approach: The last few strides before an obstacle or jump.

balance: The result of a well-schooled horse who carries himself without leaning on the reins (see also self-carriage).

bosal: A type of hackamore made from braided rawhide.

canter: A three-beat gait where the fore and hind legs on one side are in advance of those on the other side and with a definite moment of suspension where all feet are off the ground.

cavaletti: A low, small jump consisting of a single pole.

cavesson: A flat noseband used mainly for appearance because it does not influence the horse. A longeing cavesson is a leather or webbing halter with rings on the front of the noseband on which to attach a longe line.

closing the hands: Literally closing your hands to shorten the reins and restrict forward movement.

collection: Moving with shorter, more elevated strides.

contact: The link from the rider's hands to the bit of the horse, which should be elastic rather than rigid. Ideally, the impulsion from the rider's legs causes the horse to step forward and reach into the bit contact rather than the rider having to pull the horse into his/her hands.

curb bit: A bit usually with cheeks or shanks for leverage and a curb chain. Western horses are usually ridden in curb bits "off contact" with the reins loose.

diagonal: The motion of the horse in trot with diagonal pairs of legs (e.g., right fore and left hind) moving together. In rising trot (or posting) in a circle, the rider should sit as the outside foreleg (nearest the rail/wall) moves backward.

disunited: When a horse changes leg in canter, but with one leg leading in front and the opposite leg behind, which is very uncomfortable.

endurance: A timed competition over long distances and varied terrain.

extension: Encouraging the horse to move with longer strides.

flash noseband: A type of tie-down noseband. Others are called drop and grackle nosebands.

forehand: The neck, shoulders, and forelegs. Horses that are "on the forehand" can feel heavy in your hands and have to be schooled to carry more weight on the hind legs.

forward seat: Leaning forward with the rider's seat lifted out of the saddle and weight taken by the knees and balls of the feet. This position is used when galloping and jumping.

gait: The pace or specific pattern of footfalls, e.g., walk, trot. Different breeds and styles of riding have different gaits.

gallop: The fastest pace when the horse really lengthens his frame to cover the ground.

hack: To go out for a ride, a trail ride.

hackamore: A bitless bridle.

jog: A pace in Western riding similar to a slow trot.

light/heavy seat: How the rider distributes his/her weight in the saddle to influence the horse.

lope: A gait in Western riding similar to canter.

longeing: Exercising a horse in a circle from the ground with the horse attached to the handler via a long rope.

martingale: A piece of tack that helps to prevent the horse from throwing his head up too high. A standing martingale runs from noseband to girth. A running martingale runs from the reins to the girth.

napping: The resistance or stubbornness displayed by some horses that dislike leaving familiar territory or other horses.

neck reining: The technique used in Western riding to steer a horse with a loose rein.

outline: The line along the top of the horse from face to hind leg and the shape he makes when ridden. Ideally, you are seeking an outline that is rounded along the neck from poll to withers and along the back from withers to hindquarters.

"put your legs on": Squeezing with your calves and heels against the horse's sides.

rein-back: The motion of a horse stepping backwards. His legs move in diagonal pairs.

releasing: Allowing the horse more freedom in the rein contact to extend his neck or move faster.

restricting: Opposite of releasing the contact – the rider holds the contact to limit the forward movement.

self-carriage: The result of a horse that moves with his hindquarters underneath him and lightness of forehand, which facilitates balanced, elevated paces.

severe tack: Any tack, gadgets, or bits that can cause pain as a method of training or control.

short contact: The reins from bit to hand are short, meaning the horse is held.

tie-down: Any noseband that prevents a horse from opening his mouth.

transitions: The stage between one pace and another.

trot: A two-beat gait where the legs move in diagonal pairs. It can be ridden sitting or rising (posting).

walk: A slow four-beat gait.

walking in hand: Leading a horse from the ground.

Index

Note: Page numbers set in *italic type* refer to captions to pictures; page numbers set in **bold type** indicate the main subject reference.

Index and Picture Credits

Picture Credits

Unless otherwise credited below, all the photographs that appear in this book were taken by **Neil Sutherland** and **Mark Burch** especially for Interpet Publishing.

Mark Chapman: 4.

Nathan Haynes/NRH Photography
(www.nrhphotography.co.uk)**:** 49 top, 50 top right, 50 bottom right, 51 bottom center.

iStockphoto.com:
4loops: 48.
Emmanuelle Bonzami: 9 bottom left.
Alexander Briel: 64 bottom.
Barry Crossley: 26 top right, 33 bottom right, 72 top right, 75 top center, 78.
Hedda Gjerpen: Cover main image, 2, 3 left, 3 top right, 11 top left, 37 top, 41 left, 83 bottom right, 92.
Margo Harrison: 83 top right.
Anja Hild: 7 bottom, 68 left.
Rick Hyman: 40, 77 bottom right, 85 bottom left.
Kai Koehler: 35 top center.
Holly Kuchera: 11 top right.
Craig Lister: 80 top right, 81 bottom right.
Tina Lorien: 91 top right.
Markanja: 84 bottom right, 90 bottom right.
Mary Morgan: 33 bottom left.
John Rich: 56 top, 90 top right.
Nick Schlax: 8 top center.
Victoria Short: 50 bottom left.

Joshua Smith: 14 bottom left.
Lori Sparkia: 35 bottom right.
Chase Swift: 85 bottom right.
R. Sherwood Veith: 16 top.
Roland Vidmar: 39 top left.
Deanna Witzel: 1.
Zastavkin: 22 bottom.

Doreen Phillips: 95.

Shutterstock.com:
Pavel Bortel: 59 bottom center.
Nicola Gavin: 72-73 bottom.
Margo Harrison: 60 left.
Jeanne Hatch: 15 bottom left.
Ron Hilton: 51 top.
Mikhail Evgenevich Kondrashov: 60 right.
Holly Kuchera: 9 bottom right.
Brad Sauter: 91 bottom right.
Eline Spek: 90 bottom left.
Gordon Swanson: 8 bottom center.

Warning

Riding is a hazardous pastime. Horses are unpredictable, powerful animals and even something as simple as leading a horse in from a field can potentially be dangerous. Never underestimate the situation and think ahead. It is advisable to carry a mobile phone and always wear a hard hat and protective clothing when riding. Seek help if you are unsure about any aspect of horsecare or equitation.

Published by
Interpet Publishing
Vincent Lane,
Dorking,
Surrey RH4 3YX,
England
Editor: Philip de Ste. Croix
Designer: Philip Clucas MCDS
Photographers: Neil Sutherland and Mark Burch
Diagram artwork: Maggie Raynor
Index: Amanda O'Neill
Production management:
Consortium, Suffolk
Print production: Sino Publishing House Ltd, Hong Kong.

Disclaimer

The information and recommendations in this book are given without any guarantees on behalf of the author and publisher, who disclaim any liability with the use of this material.